NINJA SPEEDI COOKBOOK UK FOR BEGINNERS 2023

Quick and Delicious Recipes with 30-Day Meal Plan for Busy People to Speedi Meals, Air Fry, Bake/Roast, Slow Cook and Dehydrate on a Budget

Kai Faulkner

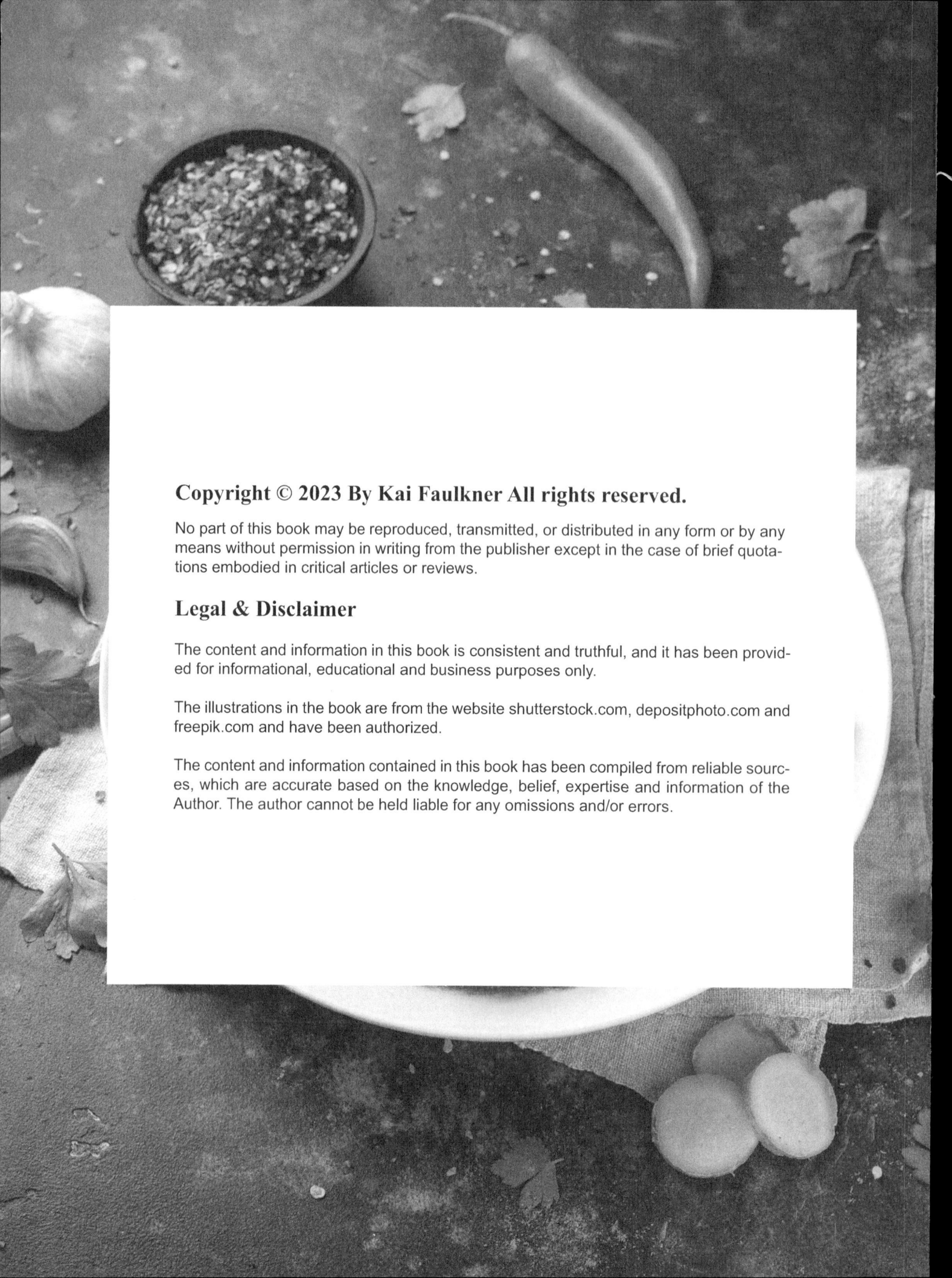

Copyright © 2023 By Kai Faulkner All rights reserved.

No part of this book may be reproduced, transmitted, or distributed in any form or by any means without permission in writing from the publisher except in the case of brief quotations embodied in critical articles or reviews.

Legal & Disclaimer

The content and information in this book is consistent and truthful, and it has been provided for informational, educational and business purposes only.

The illustrations in the book are from the website shutterstock.com, depositphoto.com and freepik.com and have been authorized.

The content and information contained in this book has been compiled from reliable sources, which are accurate based on the knowledge, belief, expertise and information of the Author. The author cannot be held liable for any omissions and/or errors.

Table of Content

Introduction ·· 1

CHAPTER 1 ABOUT THE NINJA SPEEDI RAPID COOKER AND AIR FRYER ·· 2

Benefits of Ninja Speedi Rapid Cooker and Air Fryer · 2
Smart Switch and Operating Buttons ····················· 3
Understanding the Functions ······························· 3
Cleaning and maintenance ································· 4
Troubleshooting ·· 5
Conclusion ··· 5

Chapter 2 SPEEDI MEALS ·· 6

Beef Meatballs and Pea Rice ······························ 7
Healthy Quinoa with Beef Strips ·························· 7
Beef Short Ribs with Cauliflower Rice ··················· 8
Simple Lamb Chops with Quinoa and Chickpea ······· 8
Mustard Lamb Loin Chops and Broccoli Pasta ········· 9
Lamb Loin Chops and Barley with Mushroom ·········· 9
Citrus Pork Roast and Spinach Rice ····················· 10
Chinese Pork and Mushroom Pasta ······················ 10
Pulled Pork with Mushroom Polenta ····················· 11
Jamaican Chicken Drumsticks with Spinach Couscous ······· 11
Chinese Chicken Drumsticks with Pasta ················ 12
Sesame Chicken and Bean Rice ·························· 12
Teriyaki Salmon with Brown Rice ························· 13
Breaded Hake and Green Beans Meal ·················· 13
Spicy Prawn and Broccoli Pasta ··························· 14

Chapter 3 STEAM AIR FRY ·· 15

Cheese Broccoli Bites ·· 16
Paprika Cod ··· 16
Scallops with Capers Sauce ································ 17
Cajun-Style Salmon Burgers ······························· 17
Crunchy Cod Nuggets ·· 18
Pork Tenderloin with Bell Peppers ························ 18
Cheese Stuffed Bell Peppers ······························· 19
Buttered Sweetcorn on the Cob ··························· 19
Honey Sriracha Chicken Wings ··························· 20
Beef and Carrot Meatballs ·································· 20
Italian Sausage Meatballs ··································· 21
Cheddar Turkey Burgers ····································· 21
Cheddar Turkey Burgers ····································· 22
Portabella Pizza Treat ·· 22
Chicken with Pineapple and Peach ······················· 23
Glazed Brussels Sprouts ···································· 23

Chapter 4 STEAM BAKE ·· 24

Savory Tuna Cakes ·· 25
Mushroom and Bell Pepper Pizza ························· 25
Honey Pumpkin Bread ······································· 26
Bacon and Spinach Cups ···································· 26
Beef and Spinach Rolls ······································ 27
Icing Strawberry Cupcakes ································· 27
Parmesan Sausage Muffins ································ 28
Peanut Butter Banana Bread ······························· 28
Nutty Courgette Bread ······································· 29
Prawn Burgers ·· 29
Creamy Cheese Soufflé ······································ 30
Eggless Spinach and Bacon Quiche ····················· 30
Vanilla Pecan Pie ··· 31
Walnut Chocolate Cake ······································ 31
Chocolate Cherry Turnovers ································ 32

Chapter 5 AIR FRY ·· 33

Raspberry Wontons ··· 34
Breaded Flounder with Lemon ····························· 34
Jerk Chicken Leg Quarters ·································· 35
Herbed Radishes ··· 35
Beef Steak Fingers ·· 36
Buttermilk Paprika Chicken ································· 36
Easy Crispy Prawns ··· 37
Air Fried Baby Back Ribs ···································· 37
Potato and Bacon Nuggets ·································· 38
Herbed Beef ··· 38
Almond-Crusted Chicken Nuggets ························ 39
Apple Dumplings with Sultana ····························· 39
Crispy Artichoke Hearts ······································ 40
Air Fried Chicken Tenders ·································· 40
Chilli Fingerling Potatoes ···································· 41

Chapter 6 BAKE/ROAST — 42

- Balsamic Asparagus with Almond — 43
- Roasted Aubergine Slices — 43
- Easy Roasted Salmon — 44
- Crispy Cod Cakes with Salad Greens — 44
- Spiced Turkey Tenderloin — 45
- Roasted Chicken Breast with Garlic — 45
- Simple Mexican Pork Chops — 46
- Chili Breaded Pork Chops — 46
- Pear and Apple Crisp — 47
- Cinnamon and Pecan Pie — 47
- Beef Loin with Herbs — 48
- Lamb Chops with Bulb Garlic — 48
- Classic Shortbread Fingers — 49
- Buttered Striploin Steak — 49
- Tasty Mixed Nuts — 49

Chapter 7 DEHYDRATE — 50

- 6-Hour Dehydrated Tomatoes — 51
- 8-Hour Dehydrated Asparagus — 51
- Crunchy Dehydrated Brussels Sprouts — 52
- Crispy Dehydrated Aubergine Slices — 52
- Tangy Dehydrated Mango Slices — 53
- Crispy Dehydrated Banana Chips — 53
- Crunchy Dehydrated Carrot Slices — 54
- Dehydrated Dragon Fruit — 54
- Crunchy Dehydrated Olives — 55
- Dehydrated Kiwi Fruit — 55
- Dehydrated Strawberry Slices — 55
- Sweet and Spicy Pepper Beef Jerky — 56
- Smoky Salmon Jerky — 56
- Sweet and Sour Chicken Jerky — 57
- Spicy Sriracha Turkey Jerky — 57

Chapter 8 SEARSAUTÉ — 58

- Cranberry Beef Stir-Fry with Veggies — 59
- New England Fried Chips and Fried Fish — 59
- Salt and Pepper Prawn — 60
- Sichuan Pork and Bell Pepper with Peanuts — 60
- Corned Beef — 61
- Ginger Lentil Stew — 61
- Sesame Asparagus — 62
- Little Bay Yellow Curry — 62
- Thai Basil Pork Bowls — 63
- Hoisin Tofu — 63
- Chicken Pomegranate Stew — 64
- Garlic Kimchi Chicken and Cabbage — 64
- Brussels Sprouts with Pistachios — 65
- Lime Lamb and Scallions — 65
- Sichuan Cumin-Spiced Lamb — 66

Chapter 9 SLOW COOK — 67

- Peach Brown Betty with Cranberries — 68
- Mustard Beef Brisket — 68
- Moroccan Beef Tagine and Carrot — 69
- Chicken Breast with Artichokes and Bell Pepper — 69
- Healthy Spinach Porridge — 70
- Vegan Quinoa Egg Casserole — 70
- Thai Chicken with Greens — 71
- Salmon Vegetables Chowder — 71
- Italian Beetroots and Tomato — 72
- Tilapia and Spinach Risotto — 72
- Honey Pork Chops and Carrot — 73
- Sultana Carrot Pudding — 73
- Curried Pork Chop with Pepper and Onion — 73
- Traditional Chicken Provençal — 74
- Healthy Beef Stroganoff — 74

APPENDIX 1: 30-DAY MEAL PLAN — 75
APPENDIX 2: NINJA SPEEDI TIMETABLE — 78
APPENDIX 3: RECIPES INDEX — 83

INTRODUCTION

Cooking has always been one of my passions, but there are times when I simply don't have the luxury of spending hours in the kitchen. That's why I was thrilled when I discovered the Ninja Speedi Rapid Cooker and Air Fryer. It's a kitchen appliance that has revolutionized the way I cook, making meal prep faster and more convenient than ever before.

In this cookbook, I'm excited to share some of my favorite recipes that I've created using this amazing kitchen gadget. From breakfast to dinner, and everything in between, these recipes are sure to impress even the pickiest eaters.

I hope that this cookbook will inspire you to try new recipes and experiment with the Ninja Speedi Rapid Cooker and Air Fryer. Whether you're a busy professional, a student, or a parent on the go, this appliance is a game-changer in the kitchen. So, let's get cooking!

CHAPTER 1:
ABOUT THE NINJA SPEEDI RAPID COOKER AND AIR FRYER

The Ninja Speedi Rapid Cooker and Air Fryer is a versatile kitchen appliance that can help you cook delicious meals quickly and easily. With its innovative design, this appliance combines the functions of an air fryer, slow cooker, and multiple cooking modes in one convenient device.

This appliance has a large capacity, making it ideal for families or anyone who enjoys cooking for groups. It also features Speedi Meals function, which combines steam and convection heat to create fluffy grains or al dente pasta, tender vegetables, and crispy mains – all at once.

In addition to its versatility, the Ninja Speedi Rapid Cooker and Air Fryer is also easy to use and clean. Its intuitive controls and clear display make it simple to select the right cooking mode and adjust the cooking time and temperature as needed. And when you're finished cooking, the non-stick cooking pot and accessories can be easily removed and cleaned in the dishwasher.

Overall, the Ninja Speedi Rapid Cooker and Air Fryer is a great addition to any kitchen, offering convenience, versatility, and delicious results with every use.

Benefits of Ninja Speedi Rapid Cooker and Air Fryer

Not only is the Ninja Speedi Rapid Cooker and Air Fryer versatile and easy to use, it also offers a range of benefits that can make meal preparation a breeze. Here are some of the advantages of this appliance:

- **Saves time**

With its rapid cooking technology, the Ninja Speedi Rapid Cooker and Air Fryer can cook food up to 60% faster than conventional cooking methods, helping you to save time.

- **Versatile**

This appliance can be used for a variety of cooking methods, including air frying, roasting, baking, and dehydrating, making it a versatile addition to any kitchen.

- **Healthier cooking**

The Ninja Speedi Rapid Cooker and Air Fryer uses little to no oil when air frying, resulting in healthier and lower-fat meals.

- **Easy to use**

With its intuitive and user-friendly controls, this appliance is easy to operate, even for those who are not accustomed to cooking.

- **Convenient cleaning**

The non-stick coating on the cooking surfaces of the Ninja Speedi Rapid Cooker and Air Fryer makes it easy to clean up after use.

- **Large capacity**

With a capacity of up to 5.7 litres, this appliance can cook large quantities of food at once, making it perfect for families or entertaining.

- **Customisable settings**

The Ninja Speedi Rapid Cooker and Air Fryer offers customisable temperature and time settings, allowing you to cook your food exactly how you like it.

- **Energy-efficient**

This appliance uses less energy than conventional ovens, making it an energy-efficient option for cooking.

Smart Switch and Operating Buttons

The Ninja Speedi Rapid Cooker and Air Fryer is equipped with a Smart Switch that makes it easy to switch between the Rapid Cooker mode and Air Fry/Hob cooking modes. To use the Smart Switch, first, make sure that the handle is pointing upwards, which unlocks the Rapid Cooker mode. The available cooking functions in this mode include Speedi Meals, Steam Air Fry, Steam Bake, and Steam. Then, you can turn the Smart Switch to the downward position to unlock the other cooking options like Grill, Air Fry, Bake/Roast, Dehydrate, Sear/Sauté, and Slow Cook.

In addition to the Smart Switch, the appliance also has several Operating Buttons that you can use to adjust the cooking temperature, cooking time, and to start or stop cooking. The POWER button is used to turn the unit off and stop all cooking functions. The left arrows located on the display can be used to adjust the cooking temperature, while the right arrows can be used to adjust the cooking time. To start cooking, press the START/STOP button. If you need to stop the current cooking function, you can also press this button. Finally, once you have selected a mode using the Smart Switch, you can use the centre arrows to scroll through the available functions until your desired function is highlighted.

Understanding the Functions

The Ninja Speedi Rapid Cooker and Air Fryer packs a range of cooking functions that can help you prepare delicious meals in no time. Let's take a closer look at each of its functions and how you can use them to elevate your cooking game.

Rapid Cooker Mode:

The Rapid Cooker mode offers four different options to choose from:

Speedi Meals: This function allows you to prepare meals quickly and easily using steam. Perfect for cooking quick meals, such as pasta or rice dishes.

Steam Air Fry: The combination of steam and air frying gives your food a crispy texture on the outside while keeping the inside moist. This function is perfect for cooking chicken, fish, and vegetables.

Steam Bake: Bake food with the added benefit of steam, resulting in a moist and tender texture. This function is ideal for baking bread, cakes, and pastries.

Steam: Perfect for steaming vegetables, fish, and other delicate foods.

Air Fry/Hob Mode:

This mode offers a range of cooking options, including:

Grill: Use this function to grill food to perfection, giving it a delicious smoky flavour. Perfect for cooking steaks, burgers, and vegetables.

Air Fry: Cook with hot air, giving your food a crispy texture without the need for added oil. This function is ideal for cooking French fries, chicken wings, and other fried foods.

Bake/Roast: Bake or roast food in the appliance, giving it a crispy texture on the outside and a moist and tender texture on the inside. Perfect for cooking roasts, casseroles, and baked dishes.

Dehydrate: This function allows you to dehydrate food, removing the moisture to preserve it for longer. This function is ideal for making beef jerky, dried fruits, and other dehydrated snacks.

Sear/Sauté: Cook meats and vegetables using high heat for a crispy exterior and tender interior. Great for cooking meats and vegetables.

Slow Cook: This function allows you to cook food slowly and evenly, making it perfect for stews, soups, and other slow-cooked dishes.

In summary, the Ninja Speedi Rapid Cooker and Air Fryer has a wide range of functions to help you cook a variety of meals quickly and easily. Each function is easy to use and can be selected using the Smart Switch and Operating Buttons. With this appliance, you can create delicious and healthy meals with minimal effort.

Cleaning and maintenance

To keep your Ninja Speedi Rapid Cooker and Air Fryer in good condition, it is important to clean and maintain it regularly. Here are some tips for cleaning and maintaining your appliance:

1. Unplug the unit and allow it to cool down before cleaning.
2. The cooking pot, Cook & Crisp tray, and condensation collector can be washed in the dishwasher for easy cleaning.
3. The accessories can also be washed by hand using warm, soapy water and a non-abrasive sponge or cloth.
4. Do not use steel wool or abrasive cleaning products, as they can damage the non-stick surface.
5. To remove stubborn stains or grease, use a non-abrasive cleaner or a mixture of baking soda and water.
6. To clean the exterior of the appliance, use a damp cloth and mild detergent. Do not immerse the appliance in water.

7. Wipe the heating element and interior of the appliance with a damp cloth or sponge. Do not use abrasive cleaners or scouring pads.
8. To prevent odors, wipe the interior of the appliance with a mixture of vinegar and water.

By following these tips, you can ensure that your Ninja Speedi Rapid Cooker and Air Fryer stays in good condition and functions properly for years to come.

Troubleshooting

If you encounter any issues when using the Ninja Speedi Rapid Cooker and Air Fryer, refer to the following tips to troubleshoot common problems:

1. How do I pressure cook?
This unit does not have a pressure cook function. Instead, use the RAPID COOKER functions to cook quickly. Refer to the recipe guide for inspiration. Progress bars will be displayed on the screen when using RAPID COOKER functions, indicating that the unit is building steam. When the unit has finished, your set cook time will begin counting down.

2. There is a lot of steam coming from the unit when using the RAPID COOKER functions.
It is normal for steam to release through the vent during cooking. Make sure to allow adequate space when using the appliance and ensure the vent is not directed towards the power cord, electrical socket or cupboards.

3. The unit is counting up rather than down.
This means that the cooking cycle is complete and the unit is in Keep Warm mode.

4. "ADD POT" error message appears on display screen.
This error message appears when the cooking pot is not inside the cooker base. Make sure that the cooking pot is properly inserted for all functions.

5. "SHUT LID" error message appears on display screen.
This error message appears when the lid is open and needs to be closed for the selected function to start.

6. "ERR" message appears.
This message indicates that the unit is not functioning properly. Please contact Customer Service at 0800 862 0453 for assistance.

Conclusion

In conclusion, the Ninja Speedi Rapid Cooker and Air Fryer is a versatile kitchen appliance that can help you create a wide range of delicious and healthy meals in a fraction of the time compared to traditional cooking methods. With its numerous functions and accessories, you can easily slow cook, roast, bake, air fry, and more.

I hope this cookbook has provided you with some inspiration and guidance on how to use your Ninja Speedi Rapid Cooker and Air Fryer to its full potential. Whether you are a busy professional, a student, or a homemaker, this appliance can simplify your cooking routine and help you prepare healthy meals for your family and friends.

Remember to always read the recipe instructions carefully and follow the safety guidelines provided in the user manual. With some practice and experimentation, you can become a master of the Ninja Speedi Rapid Cooker and Air Fryer and impress everyone with your culinary skills.

Thank you for choosing Ninja Speedi Rapid Cooker and Air Fryer as your cooking partner. I wish you happy cooking and delicious meals!

CHAPTER 2
SPEEDI MEALS

Beef Meatballs and Pea Rice

Prep: 10 minutes, Total Cook Time: 25 minutes, Steam: approx. 10 minutes, Cook: 15 minutes, Serves: 2

INGREDIENTS:

LEVEL 1 (BOTTOM OF POT)
- 180 g brown rice, rinsed
- 375 ml water
- 130 g frozen peas

LEVEL 2 (TRAY)
- 450 g beef, minced
- 60 g grated Parmesan cheese
- 15 g minced garlic
- 60 g Mozzarella cheese
- 1 tsp. freshly ground pepper

TOPPINGS:
- Tzatziki sauce
- Fresh chopped parsley

DIRECTIONS:

1. Place all Level 1 ingredients in the pot and stir to combine.
2. Pull out the legs on the Cook & Crisp tray, then place the tray in the top position in the pot.
3. In a bowl, mix all Level 2 ingredients together.
4. Roll the meat mixture into 6 generous meatballs.
5. Place the meatballs on top of the tray.
6. Close the lid and flip the SmartSwitch to RAPID COOKER.
7. Select SPEEDI MEALS, set temperature to 180°C, and set time to 15 minutes. Press START/STOP to begin cooking (the unit will steam for approx. 10 minutes, before countdown time begins).
8. When cooking is complete, remove the meatballs from the tray. Then use silicone-tipped tongs to grab the centre handle and remove the tray from the unit. Transfer the pea rice to a bowl, then top with the meatballs and toppings.
9. Serve immediately.

Healthy Quinoa with Beef Strips

Prep: 5 minutes, Total Cook Time: 22 to 25 minutes, Steam: approx. 7 to 8 minutes, Cook: 15 minutes, Serves: 2

INGREDIENTS:

LEVEL 1 (BOTTOM OF POT)
- 200 g quinoa, rinsed
- 375 ml water

LEVEL 2 (TRAY)
- 15 ml olive oil
- 2 beef steaks
- 1 tsp. dried thyme

DIRECTIONS:

1. Place all Level 1 ingredients in the pot and stir to combine well.
2. Pull out the legs on the Cook & Crisp tray, then place the tray in the top position in the pot above the quinoa.
3. Mix the Level 2 ingredients in a bowl.
4. Place the beef steaks on top of the tray in a single layer.
5. Close the lid and flip the SmartSwitch to RAPID COOKER. Select SPEEDI MEALS, set temperature to 200°C, and set time to 15 minutes. Press START/STOP to begin cooking (the unit will steam for approx. 7 to 8 minutes, before countdown time begins).
6. When cooking is complete, remove the steak from the tray. Let cool for 5 minutes and slice into 2.5 cm strips. Then use silicone tipped tongs to remove the Cook & Crisp tray. Remove quinoa to a bowl. Serve warm with the beef strips.

Beef Short Ribs with Cauliflower Rice

Prep: 20 minutes, Total Cook Time: 20 minutes, Steam: approx. 10 minutes, Cook: 10 minutes, Serves: 4

INGREDIENTS:

LEVEL 1 (BOTTOM OF POT)
- 425 g frozen riced cauliflower
- 70 g fresh kale
- 110 g shredded cheddar cheese
- 30 g salted butter, cubed
- Salt and black pepper, to taste

LEVEL 2 (TRAY)
- 900 g bone-in beef short ribs
- 30 g scallions, chopped
- 5 g fresh ginger, finely grated
- 240 ml low-sodium soy sauce
- 120 ml rice vinegar
- 15 ml Sriracha
- 25 g brown sugar
- 1 tsp. ground black pepper

TOPPINGS:
- Diced tomatoes
- Sour cream
- Guacamole

DIRECTIONS:

1. Put the ribs with all Level 2 ingredients in a resealable bag and seal the bag. Shake to coat well and refrigerate overnight.
2. Place all Level 1 ingredients in the pot and stir to combine.
3. Pull out the legs on the Cook & Crisp tray, then place the tray in the top position in the pot.
4. Remove the short ribs from resealable bag and arrange on top of the tray.
5. Close the lid and flip the SmartSwitch to RAPID COOKER.
6. Select SPEEDI MEALS, set temperature to 200°C, and set time to 10 minutes. Press START/STOP to begin cooking (the unit will steam for approx. 10 minutes, before countdown time begins).
7. When cooking is complete, remove the short ribs from the tray. Then use silicone-tipped tongs to grab the centre handle and remove the tray from the unit. Transfer the cauliflower rice and kale to a bowl, then top with the short ribs and desired toppings.

Simple Lamb Chops with Quinoa and Chickpea

Prep: 15 minutes, Total Cook Time: 25 minutes, Steam: approx. 10 minutes, Cook: 15 minutes, Serves: 2

INGREDIENTS:

LEVEL 1 (BOTTOM OF POT)
- 200 g quinoa, rinsed
- 80 g tinned chickpeas
- 375 ml water or stock

LEVEL 2 (TRAY)
- 4 (115 g each) lamb chops
- Salt and black pepper, to taste
- 15 ml olive oil

TOPPINGS:
- Sour cream
- Pesto

DIRECTIONS:

1. Place all Level 1 ingredients in the pot and stir to combine.
2. Pull out the legs on the Cook & Crisp tray, then place the tray in the top position in the pot.
3. Mix the olive oil, salt, and black pepper in a large bowl and add chops. Arrange the chops on top of the tray.
4. Close the lid and flip the SmartSwitch to RAPID COOKER.
5. Select SPEEDI MEALS, set temperature to 190°C, and set time to 15 minutes. Press START/STOP to begin cooking (the unit will steam for approx. 10 minutes, before countdown time begins).
6. When cooking is complete, remove the chops from the tray. Then use silicone-tipped tongs to grab the centre handle and remove the tray from the unit. Transfer the quinoa and chickpea to a bowl, then top with the chops and desired toppings.

Mustard Lamb Loin Chops and Broccoli Pasta

Prep: 15 minutes, Total Cook Time: 25 minutes, Steam: approx. 10 minutes, Cook: 15 minutes, Serves: 4

INGREDIENTS:

LEVEL 1 (BOTTOM OF POT)
- 225 g Fusilli pasta
- 120 ml Basil Pesto
- 60 g broccoli
- 500 ml water

LEVEL 2 (TRAY)
- 8 (115 g each) lamb loin chops
- 30 ml Dijon mustard
- 15 ml fresh lemon juice
- 2 ml olive oil
- 1 tsp. dried tarragon
- Salt and black pepper, to taste

TOPPINGS:
- Sesame seeds
- Tzatziki

DIRECTIONS:

1. Place all Level 1 ingredients in the pot and stir to combine.
2. Pull out the legs on the Cook & Crisp tray, then place the tray in the top position in the pot.
3. Mix the mustard, lemon juice, oil, tarragon, salt, and black pepper in a large bowl.
4. Coat the chops generously with the mustard mixture and arrange on top of the tray.
5. Close the lid and flip the SmartSwitch to RAPID COOKER.
6. Select SPEEDI MEALS, set temperature to 190°C, and set time to 15 minutes. Press START/STOP to begin cooking (the unit will steam for approx. 10 minutes, before countdown time begins).
7. When cooking is complete, remove the chops from the tray. Then use silicone-tipped tongs to grab the centre handle and remove the tray from the unit. Transfer the pasta and broccoli to a bowl, then top with the chops and desired toppings.

Lamb Loin Chops and Barley with Mushroom

Prep: 20 minutes, Total Cook Time: 27 minutes, Steam: approx. 10 minutes, Cook: 17 minutes, Serves: 4

INGREDIENTS:

LEVEL 1 (BOTTOM OF POT)
- 200 g cooked hulled barley
- 150 g mushrooms, sliced
- 500 ml cheesy vegetable sauce
- 500 ml water

LEVEL 2 (TRAY)
- 8 (100 g each) bone-in lamb loin chops, trimmed
- 3 garlic cloves, crushed
- 15 ml fresh lemon juice
- 5 ml olive oil
- Salt and black pepper, to taste

TOPPINGS:
- Salsa
- Tzatziki

DIRECTIONS:

1. Place all Level 1 ingredients in the pot and stir to combine.
2. Pull out the legs on the Cook & Crisp tray, then place the tray in the top position in the pot.
3. Mix the garlic, lemon juice, oil, salt, and black pepper in a large bowl.
4. Coat the chops generously with the herb mixture and arrange the chops on top of the tray.
5. Close the lid and flip the SmartSwitch to RAPID COOKER.
6. Select SPEEDI MEALS, set temperature to 190°C, and set time to 17 minutes. Press START/STOP to begin cooking (the unit will steam for approx. 10 minutes, before countdown time begins).
7. When cooking is complete, remove the chops from the tray. Then use silicone-tipped tongs to grab the centre handle and remove the tray from the unit. Transfer the barley and mushroom to a bowl, then top with the chops and desired toppings.

Citrus Pork Roast and Spinach Rice

Prep: 20 minutes, Total Cook Time: 45 minutes, Steam: approx. 10 minutes, Cook: 35 minutes, Serves: 4

INGREDIENTS:

LEVEL 1 (BOTTOM OF POT)
- 190 g Arborio rice, rinsed
- 1 L water
- 40 g baby spinach
- 1 tsp. coarse salt
- 1 tsp. ground black pepper

LEVEL 2 (TRAY)
- 15 ml lime juice
- 1 tbsp. orange marmalade
- 1 tsp. coarse brown mustard
- 1 tsp. curry powder
- 1 tsp. dried lemongrass
- 900 g boneless pork loin roast
- Salt and ground black pepper, to taste
- Cooking spray

DIRECTIONS:

1. Place all Level 1 ingredients in the pot and stir to combine.
2. Pull out the legs on the Cook & Crisp tray, then place the tray in the top position in the pot. Spray the tray with cooking spray
3. Mix the lime juice, marmalade, mustard, curry powder, and lemongrass.
4. Rub mixture all over the surface of the pork loin. Season with salt and pepper.
5. Place the pork roast diagonally on top of the tray.
6. Close the lid and flip the SmartSwitch to RAPID COOKER.
7. Select SPEEDI MEALS, set temperature to 180°C, and set time to 35 minutes. Press START/STOP to begin cooking (the unit will steam for approx. 10 minutes, before countdown time begins).
8. When cooking is complete, remove the roast from the tray and cut into desired size slices. Then use silicone-tipped tongs to grab the centre handle and remove the tray from the unit. Transfer the rice and spinach to a bowl, then top with the roast.
9. Serve hot.

Chinese Pork and Mushroom Pasta

Prep: 20 minutes, Total Cook Time: 24 minutes, Steam: approx. 10 minutes, Cook: 14 minutes, Serves: 4

INGREDIENTS:

LEVEL 1 (BOTTOM OF POT)
- 15 ml oil
- 225 g mushrooms, minced
- ½ tsp. coarse salt
- ½ tsp. black ground pepper
- 225 g uncooked spaghetti pasta
- 500 ml water
- 120 ml pesto
- 30 g grated Parmesan cheese

LEVEL 2 (TRAY)
- 60 ml coconut oil
- 4 garlic cloves, minced
- 1 tbsp. fresh ginger
- 4 boneless pork chops
- 30 ml soy sauce
- Salt and pepper, to taste

DIRECTIONS:

1. Place all Level 1 ingredients in the pot and stir to combine.
2. Pull out the legs on the Cook & Crisp tray, then place the tray in the top position in the pot.
3. In a large bowl, mix the pork chops with the remaining ingredients. Marinade for 5 minutes. Place the pork chops on top of the tray.
4. Close the lid and flip the SmartSwitch to RAPID COOKER.
5. Select SPEEDI MEALS, set temperature to 190°C, and set time to 14 minutes. Press START/STOP to begin cooking (the unit will steam for approx. 10 minutes, before countdown time begins).
6. When cooking is complete, remove the pork chops from the tray. Then use silicone-tipped tongs to grab the centre handle and remove the tray from the unit. Transfer the mushroom pasta to a bowl, then top with the pork chops.
7. Serve hot.

Pulled Pork with Mushroom Polenta

Prep: 12 minutes, Total Cook Time: 40-45 minutes, Steam: approx. 10-15 minutes, Cook: 30 minutes, Serves: 4

INGREDIENTS:

LEVEL 1 (BOTTOM OF POT)
- 170 g yellow cornmeal
- 1 L vegetable broth
- 15 g butter
- 2 portobello mushrooms caps, finely chopped
- 1 tsp. onion powder
- 1 tsp. coarse salt
- 1 tsp. freshly ground black pepper

LEVEL 2 (TRAY)
- 680 g pork shoulder
- 1 tsp. cinnamon
- 2 tsps. garlic powder
- 75 ml coconut oil
- 1 tsp. cumin powder
- Salt and pepper, to taste

DIRECTIONS:

1. Place all Level 1 ingredients in the pot and stir to combine.
2. Pull out the legs on the Cook & Crisp tray, then place the tray in the top position in the pot.
3. Mix all Level 2 ingredients in a large bowl and stir to combine well. Place the pork on top of the tray.
4. Close the lid and flip the SmartSwitch to RAPID COOKER.
5. Select SPEEDI MEALS, set temperature to 190°C, and set time to 30 minutes. Press START/STOP to begin cooking (the unit will steam for approx. 10 to 15 minutes, before countdown time begins).
6. When cooking is complete, remove the pork from the tray and and shred with two forks. Then use silicone-tipped tongs to grab the centre handle and remove the tray from the unit. Transfer the Mushroom Polenta to a bowl, then top with the pork.

Jamaican Chicken Drumsticks with Spinach Couscous

Prep: 15 minutes, Total Cook Time: 30-35 minutes, Steam: approx. 10-15 minutes, Cook: 20 minutes, Serves: 4

INGREDIENTS:

LEVEL 1 (BOTTOM OF POT)
- 15 g butter
- 180 g couscous
- 625 ml vegetable broth
- 30 g chopped spinach, blanched
- 1½ tomatoes, chopped

LEVEL 2 (TRAY)
- 4 (140-170 g each) chicken drumsticks
- 1 tbsp. Jamaican curry powder
- 1 tsp. salt
- ½ medium onion, diced
- ½ tsp. dried thyme

DIRECTIONS:

1. Place all Level 1 ingredients in the pot and stir to combine.
2. Pull out the legs on the Cook & Crisp tray, then place the tray in the top position in the pot.
3. Sprinkle the salt and curry powder over the chicken drumsticks. Place the chicken on top of the tray, along with the remaining ingredients.
4. Close the lid and flip the SmartSwitch to RAPID COOKER.
5. Select SPEEDI MEALS, set temperature to 200°C, and set time to 20 minutes. Press START/STOP to begin cooking (the unit will steam for approx. 10 to 15 minutes, before countdown time begins).
6. When cooking is complete, remove the chicken from the tray. Then use silicone-tipped tongs to grab the centre handle and remove the tray from the unit. Transfer the couscous and vegetables to a bowl, then top with the chicken.
7. Serve warm.

Chinese Chicken Drumsticks with Pasta

Prep: 20 minutes, Total Cook Time: 30-35 minutes, Steam: approx. 10-15 minutes, Cook: 20 minutes, Serves: 4

INGREDIENTS:

LEVEL 1 (BOTTOM OF POT)
- 225 g penne pasta
- 1 (410 g) tinned alfredo sauce
- 115 g frozen cauliflower florets
- 300 ml water or stock

LEVEL 2 (TRAY)
- 4 (170 g) chicken drumsticks
- 125 g corn flour
- 1 tbsp. oyster sauce
- 1 tsp. light soy sauce
- ½ tsp. sesame oil
- 1 g Chinese five spice powder
- Salt and white pepper, as required

TOPPINGS:
- Fresh herbs
- Salsa
- Guacamole
- Sour cream

DIRECTIONS:

1. Place all Level 1 ingredients in the pot and stir to combine.
2. Pull out the legs on the Cook & Crisp tray, then place the tray in the top position in the pot.
3. Mix the sauces, oil, five spice powder, salt, and black pepper in a bowl.
4. Rub the chicken drumsticks with marinade and refrigerate for about 30 minutes.
5. Arrange the drumsticks on top of the tray.
6. Close the lid and flip the SmartSwitch to RAPID COOKER.
7. Select SPEEDI MEALS, set temperature to 200°C, and set time to 20 minutes. Press START/STOP to begin cooking (the unit will steam for approx. 10 to 15 minutes, before countdown time begins).
8. When cooking is complete, remove the chicken drumsticks from the tray. Then use silicone-tipped tongs to grab the centre handle and remove the tray from the unit. Transfer the pasta and cauliflower to a bowl, then top with the chicken drumsticks and desired toppings.

Sesame Chicken and Bean Rice

Prep: 20 minutes, Total Cook Time: 25 minutes, Steam: approx. 10 minutes, Cook: 15 minutes, Serves: 4

INGREDIENTS:

LEVEL 1 (BOTTOM OF POT)
- 200 g white rice, rinsed
- 240 g tinned black beans, drained
- 500 ml water

LEVEL 2 (TRAY)
- 360 ml soy sauce
- 2 tsps. chicken seasoning
- 680 g chicken breasts or thighs

TOPPING:
- 20 g toasted sesame seeds

DIRECTIONS:

1. Place all Level 1 ingredients in the pot and stir to combine.
2. Pull out the legs on the Cook & Crisp tray, then place the tray in the top position in the pot.
3. In a large bowl, mix the chicken with soy sauce and chicken seasoning. Marinade for about 30 minutes. Place the chicken on top of the tray.
4. Close the lid and flip the SmartSwitch to RAPID COOKER.
5. Select SPEEDI MEALS, set temperature to 200°C, and set time to 15 minutes. Press START/STOP to begin cooking (the unit will steam for approx. 10 minutes, before countdown time begins).
6. When cooking is complete, remove the chicken from the tray. Then use silicone-tipped tongs to grab the centre handle and remove the tray from the unit. Transfer the rice and beans to a bowl, then top with the chicken and sesame seeds.

Teriyaki Salmon with Brown Rice

Prep: 20 minutes, Total Cook Time: 30-35 minutes, Steam: approx. 10-15 minutes, Cook: 20 minutes, Serves: 4

INGREDIENTS:

LEVEL 1 (BOTTOM OF POT)
- 30 ml olive oil
- 1 L water
- 400 g easy-cooked brown rice, rinsed
- Salt, to taste

LEVEL 2 (TRAY)
- 450 g salmon fillets
- 110 g packed light brown sugar
- 120 ml rice vinegar
- 120 ml soy sauce
- 1 tbsp. cornflour
- 1 tsp. minced ginger
- ¼ tsp. garlic powder

TOPPINGS:
- Sour cream
- Tzatziki

DIRECTIONS:

1. Place all Level 1 ingredients in the pot and stir to combine.
2. Pull out the legs on the Cook & Crisp tray, then place the tray in the top position in the pot.
3. Whisk together the remaining ingredients except the salmon fillets in a small bowl until well combined. Pour the mixture over the salmon fillets, turning to coat. Place the fillets on top of the tray.
4. Close the lid and flip the SmartSwitch to RAPID COOKER.
5. Select SPEEDI MEALS, set temperature to 180°C, and set time to 14 minutes. Press START/STOP to begin cooking (the unit will steam for approx. 10 minutes, before countdown time begins).
6. When cooking is complete, remove the salmon from the tray. Then use silicone-tipped tongs to grab the centre handle and remove the tray from the unit. Transfer the rice to a bowl, then top with the salmon and toppings.

Breaded Hake and Green Beans Meal

Prep: 25 minutes, Total Cook Time: 22 minutes, Steam: approx. 10 minutes, Cook: 12 minutes, Serves: 2

INGREDIENTS:

LEVEL 1 (BOTTOM OF POT)
- 180 g white rice, rinsed
- 500 ml water
- 170 g green beans

LEVEL 2 (TRAY)
- 1 egg
- 110 g breadcrumbs
- 4 (170 g) hake fillets
- 1 lemon, cut into wedges
- 30 ml vegetable oil

DIRECTIONS:

1. Place all Level 1 ingredients in the pot and stir to combine.
2. Pull out the legs on the Cook & Crisp tray, then place the tray in the top position in the pot.
3. Whisk the egg in a shallow bowl and mix breadcrumbs and oil in another bowl.
4. Dip hake fillets into the whisked egg and then, dredge in the breadcrumb mixture.
5. Place the hake fillets on top of the tray.
6. Close the lid and flip the SmartSwitch to RAPID COOKER.
7. Select SPEEDI MEALS, set temperature to 180°C, and set time to 12 minutes. Press START/STOP to begin cooking (the unit will steam for approx. 10 minutes, before countdown time begins).
8. When cooking is complete, remove the hake fillets from the tray. Then use silicone-tipped tongs to grab the centre handle and remove the tray from the unit. Transfer the rice and green beans to a bowl, then top with the hake fillets. Serve garnished with lemon wedges.

Spicy Prawn and Broccoli Pasta

Prep: 25 minutes, Total Cook Time: 22 minutes, Steam: approx. 10 minutes, Cook: 12 minutes, Serves: 2

INGREDIENTS:

- LEVEL 1 (BOTTOM OF POT)
- 1 box (225 g) legume-based pasta
- 300 g broccoli, cut into 2.5 cm florets
- 750 ml water
- LEVEL 2 (TRAY)
- 450 g prawns, peeled and deveined
- 30 ml olive oil
- 1 tsp. old bay seasoning
- ½ tsp. red chili flakes
- ½ tsp. smoked paprika
- ½ tsp. cayenne pepper
- Salt, as required

DIRECTIONS:

1. Place all Level 1 ingredients in the pot and stir to combine.
2. Pull out the legs on the Cook & Crisp tray, then place the tray in the top position in the pot.
3. Mix prawns with olive oil and other seasonings in a large bowl.
4. Arrange the prawns on top of tray in a single layer.
5. Close the lid and flip the SmartSwitch to RAPID COOKER.
6. Select SPEEDI MEALS, set temperature to 180°C, and set time to 12 minutes. Press START/STOP to begin cooking (the unit will steam for approx. 10 minutes, before countdown time begins).
7. When cooking is complete, remove the prawns from the tray. Then use silicone-tipped tongs to grab the centre handle and remove the tray from the unit. Transfer the broccoli pasta to a bowl, then top with the prawns.
8. Serve hot.

CHAPTER 3
STEAM AIR FRY

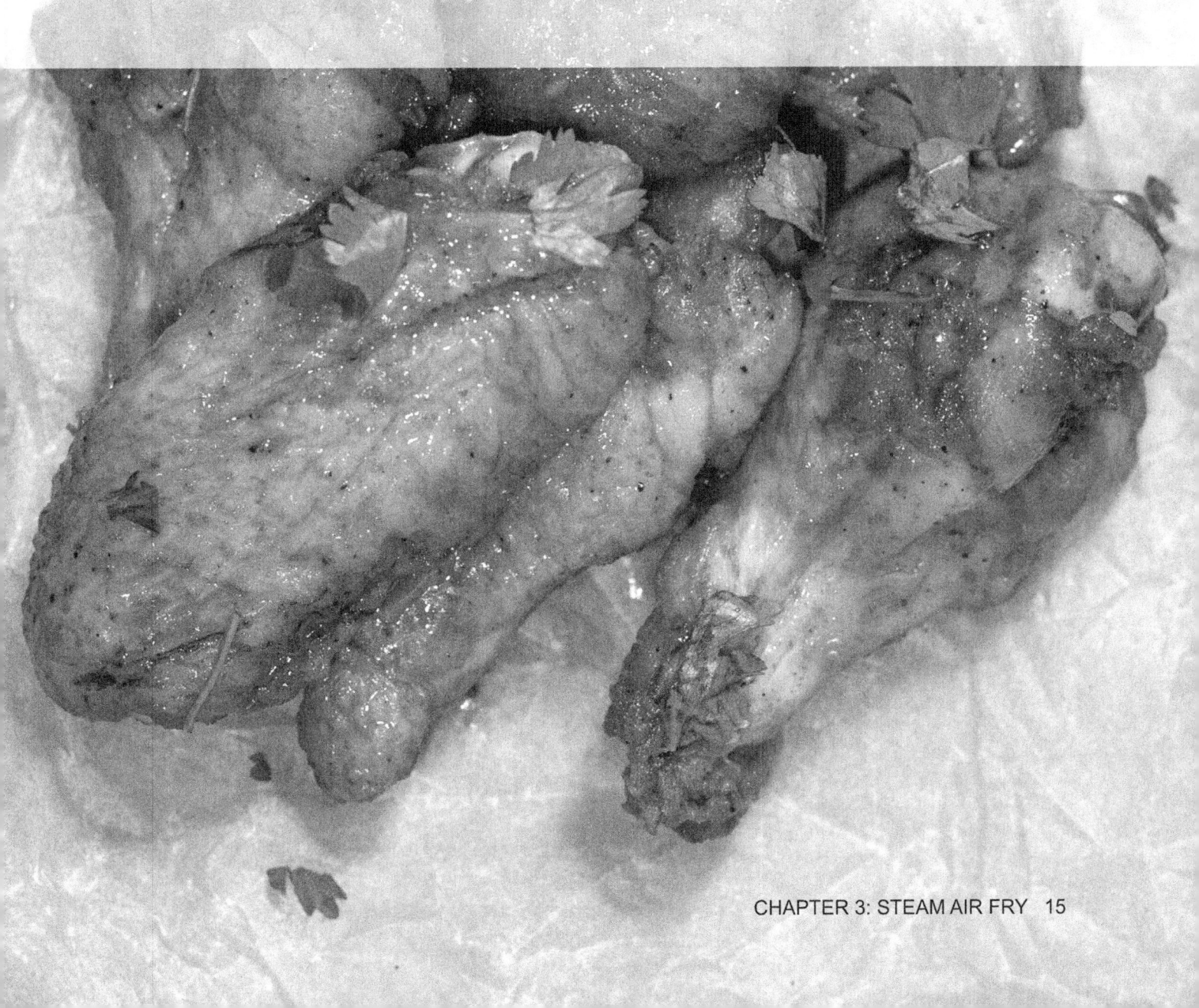

Cheese Broccoli Bites

Prep: 15 minutes, Total Cook Time: 19 minutes, Steam: approx. 4 minutes, Cook: 15 minutes, Makes: 10 bites

INGREDIENTS:

- 125 ml water, for steaming
- 400 g broccoli florets
- 2 eggs, beaten
- 125 g cheddar cheese, grated
- 25 g Parmesan cheese, grated
- 120 g panko breadcrumbs
- Salt and black pepper, to taste

DIRECTIONS:

1. Pour 125 ml water into the pot. Push in the legs on the Cook & Crisp tray, then place the tray in the bottom position in the pot.
2. Mix broccoli with rest of the ingredients and mix until well combined.
3. Make small equal-sized balls from mixture and arrange these balls in a baking pan. Refrigerate for about half an hour and then transfer into the tray.
4. Close the lid and flip the SmartSwitch to RAPID COOKER. Select STEAM AIR FRY, set temperature to 210°C and set time to 15 minutes. Press START/STOP to begin cooking (the unit will steam for approx. 4 minutes, before countdown time begins).
5. With 6 minutes remaining, open the lid and flip the broccoli with tongs. Close the lid to continue cooking.
6. Dish out to serve warm.

Paprika Cod

Prep: 10 minutes, Total Cook Time: 14 minutes, Steam: approx. 4 minutes, Cook: 10 minutes, Serves: 2

INGREDIENTS:

- 125 ml water, for steaming
- 2 (170 g) cod fillets (4-cm thick)
- 1 tsp. smoked paprika
- 1 tsp. cayenne pepper
- 1 tsp. onion powder
- 1 tsp. garlic powder
- Salt and ground black pepper, as required
- 10 ml olive oil

DIRECTIONS:

1. Pour 125 ml water into the pot. Pull out the legs on the Cook & Crisp tray, then place the tray in the top position in the pot.
2. Drizzle the cod fillets with olive oil and rub with the all the spices.
3. Arrange the cod fillets on the tray.
4. Close the lid and flip the SmartSwitch to RAPID COOKER. Select STEAM AIR FRY, set temperature to 220°C, and set time to 10 minutes. Press START/STOP to begin cooking (the unit will steam for approx. 4 minutes, before countdown time begins).
5. With 4 minutes remaining, open the lid and toss the cod fillets with tongs. Close the lid to continue cooking.
6. When cooking is complete, use tongs to remove the cod fillets from the tray and serve hot.

Scallops with Capers Sauce

Prep: 15 minutes, Total Cook Time: 10 minutes, Steam: approx. 4 minutes, Cook: 6 minutes, Serves: 2

INGREDIENTS:

- 60 ml water, for steaming
- 10 (30 g each) sea scallops, cleaned and patted very dry
- 2 tbsps. fresh parsley, finely chopped
- 2 tsps. capers, finely chopped
- Salt and ground black pepper, to taste
- 60 ml extra-virgin olive oil
- 1 tsp. fresh lemon zest, finely grated
- ½ tsp. garlic, finely chopped

DIRECTIONS:

1. Pour 60 ml water into the pot. Pull out the legs on the Cook & Crisp tray, then place the tray in the top position in the pot.
2. Season the scallops evenly with salt and black pepper. Arrange the scallops on the tray.
3. Close the lid and flip the SmartSwitch to RAPID COOKER. Select STEAM AIR FRY, set temperature to 220°C, and set time to 6 minutes. Press START/STOP to begin cooking (the unit will steam for approx. 4 minutes, before countdown time begins).
4. Mix parsley, capers, olive oil, lemon zest and garlic in a bowl.
5. Dish out the scallops in a platter and top with capers sauce.

Cajun-Style Salmon Burgers

Prep: 10 minutes, Total Cook Time: 19 minutes, Steam: approx. 4 minutes, Cook: 15 minutes, Serves: 4

INGREDIENTS:

- 125 ml water, for steaming
- 4 (210 g) tins of pink salmon in water, any skin and bones removed, drained
- 2 medium eggs, beaten
- 85 g wholemeal bread crumbs
- 60 ml light mayonnaise
- 2 tsps. Cajun seasoning
- 2 tsps. dry mustard
- 4 wholemeal burger buns
- Cooking spray

DIRECTIONS:

1. In a medium bowl, mix the salmon, egg, bread crumbs, mayonnaise, Cajun seasoning, and dry mustard. Cover with plastic wrap and refrigerate for 30 minutes.
2. Pour 125 ml water into the pot. Pull out the legs on the Cook & Crisp tray, then place the tray in the top position in the pot.
3. Shape the mixture into four 1.5 cm-thick patties about the same size as the buns.
4. Place the salmon patties on the tray and lightly spray with cooking spray.
5. Close the lid and flip the SmartSwitch to RAPID COOKER. Select STEAM AIR FRY, set temperature to 190°C, and set time to 15 minutes. Press START/STOP to begin cooking (the unit will steam for approx. 4 minutes, before countdown time begins).
6. With 7 minutes remaining, open the lid and flip the patties with tongs. Close the lid to continue cooking.
7. When cooking is complete, serve on whole-wheat buns.

Crunchy Cod Nuggets

Prep: 15 minutes, Total Cook Time: 16 minutes, Steam: approx. 4 minutes, Cook: 12 minutes, Serves: 4

INGREDIENTS:

- 125 ml water, for steaming
- 120 g plain flour
- 2 eggs
- 75 g breadcrumbs
- 450 g cod, cut into 2.5x6 cm strips
- A pinch of salt
- 30 ml olive oil

DIRECTIONS:

1. Pour 125 ml water into the pot. Pull out the legs on the Cook & Crisp tray, then place the tray in the top position in the pot.
2. Place flour in a shallow dish and whisk the eggs in a second dish.
3. Place breadcrumbs, salt, and olive oil in a third shallow dish.
4. Coat the cod strips evenly in flour and dip in the eggs.
5. Roll into the breadcrumbs evenly and arrange the nuggets on the tray.
6. Close the lid and flip the SmartSwitch to RAPID COOKER. Select STEAM AIR FRY, set temperature to 200°C, and set time to 12 minutes. Press START/STOP to begin cooking (the unit will steam for approx. 4 minutes, before countdown time begins).
7. With 6 minutes remaining, open the lid and flip the nuggets with tongs. Close the lid to continue cooking.
8. When cooking is complete, use tongs to remove the nuggets from the tray and serve warm.

Pork Tenderloin with Bell Peppers

Prep: 20 minutes, Total Cook Time: 26 minutes, Steam: approx. 4 minutes, Cook: 22 minutes, Serves: 3

INGREDIENTS:

- 250 ml water, for steaming
- 1 large red bell pepper, seeded and cut into thin strips
- 1 red onion, thinly sliced
- 300 g pork tenderloin, cut into 3 pieces
- 2 tsps. Herbs de Provence
- Salt and ground black pepper, as required
- 15 ml olive oil
- ½ tbsp. Dijon mustard

DIRECTIONS:

1. Pour 250 ml water into the pot. Pull out the legs on the Cook & Crisp tray, then place the tray in the top position in the pot.
2. Mix the bell pepper, onion, Herbs de Provence, salt, black pepper, and ½ tbsp. of oil in a bowl.
3. Rub the tenderloins evenly with mustard, salt, and black pepper and drizzle with the remaining oil.
4. Place bell pepper mixture on the tray and top with the pork tenderloin.
5. Close the lid and flip the SmartSwitch to RAPID COOKER. Select STEAM AIR FRY, set temperature to 190°C, and set time to 22 minutes. Press START/STOP to begin cooking (the unit will steam for approx. 4 minutes, before countdown time begins).
6. With 10 minutes remaining, open the lid and flip the pork with tongs. Close the lid to continue cooking.
7. When cooking is complete, dish out the pork and cut into desired size slices to serve.

Cheese Stuffed Bell Peppers

Prep: 20 minutes, Total Cook Time: 29 minutes, Steam: approx. 4 minutes, Cook: 25 minutes, Serves: 6

INGREDIENTS:

- 125 ml water, for steaming
- 6 large bell peppers, tops and seeds removed
- 1 carrot, peeled and finely chopped
- 1 potato, peeled and finely chopped
- 70 g fresh peas, shelled
- 35 g cheddar cheese, grated
- 2 garlic cloves, minced
- Salt and black pepper, to taste

DIRECTIONS:

1. Pour 125 ml water into the pot. Push in the legs on the Cook & Crisp tray, then place the tray in the bottom position in the pot.
2. Mix vegetables, garlic, salt and black pepper in a bowl.
3. Stuff the vegetable mixture in each bell pepper and arrange on the tray.
4. Close the lid and flip the SmartSwitch to RAPID COOKER. Select STEAM AIR FRY, set temperature to 190°C, and set time to 25 minutes. Press START/STOP to begin cooking (the unit will steam for approx. 4 minutes, before countdown time begins).
5. With 5 minutes remaining, open the lid and top with cheddar cheese. Close the lid to continue cooking.
6. When cooking is complete, use tongs to remove the bell peppers from the tray and serve warm.

Buttered Sweetcorn on the Cob

Prep: 10 minutes, Total Cook Time: 28 minutes, Steam: approx. 8 minutes, Cook: 20 minutes, Serves: 2

INGREDIENTS:

- 125 ml water, for steaming
- 2 sweetcorn on the cob
- 30 g butter, softened and divided
- Salt and black pepper, to taste

DIRECTIONS:

1. Pour 125 ml water into the pot. Push in the legs on the Cook & Crisp tray, then place the tray in the bottom position in the pot.
2. Season the cobs evenly with salt and black pepper and rub with 15 g butter.
3. Wrap the cobs in foil paper and arrange on the tray.
4. Close the lid and flip the SmartSwitch to RAPID COOKER. Select STEAM AIR FRY, set temperature to 160°C, and set time to 20 minutes. Press START/STOP to begin cooking (the unit will steam for approx. 8 minutes, before countdown time begins).
5. When cooking is complete, top with remaining butter. Serve warm.

Honey Sriracha Chicken Wings

Prep: 5 minutes, Total Cook Time: 29 minutes, Steam: approx. 4 minutes, Cook: 25 minutes, Serves: 4

INGREDIENTS:

- 125 ml water, for steaming
- 15 ml Sriracha hot sauce
- 15 ml honey
- 1 garlic clove, minced
- ½ tsp. coarse salt
- 8 chicken wings and drumettes

DIRECTIONS:

1. Pour 125 ml water into the pot. Push in the legs on the Cook & Crisp tray, then place the tray in the bottom position in the pot.
2. In a large bowl, whisk together the Sriracha hot sauce, honey, minced garlic, and coarse salt, then add the chicken and toss to coat. Transfer the wings to the tray.
3. Close the lid and flip the SmartSwitch to RAPID COOKER. Select STEAM AIR FRY, set temperature to 220°C, and set time to 25 minutes. Press START/STOP to begin cooking (the unit will steam for approx. 4 minutes, before countdown time begins).
4. With 10 minutes remaining, open the lid and flip the wings with tongs. Close the lid to continue cooking.
5. When cooking is complete, remove the wings and allow to cool on a wire rack for 10 minutes before serving.

Beef and Carrot Meatballs

Prep: 10 minutes, Total Cook Time: 19 minutes, Steam: approx. 4 minutes, Cook: 15 minutes, Serves: 8

INGREDIENTS:

- 125 ml water, for steaming
- 450 g beef, minced
- 2 carrots, shredded
- 1 egg, beaten
- 2 bread slices, crumbled
- 1 small onion, minced
- 500 ml pasta sauce
- 250 ml tomato sauce
- ½ tsp. garlic salt
- Pepper and salt, to taste

DIRECTIONS:

1. Pour 125 ml water into the pot. Push in the legs on the Cook & Crisp tray, then place the tray in the bottom position in the pot.
2. In a bowl, mix the minced beef, egg, carrots, crumbled bread, onion, garlic salt, pepper and salt.
3. Distribute the mixture into equal amounts and form each one into a small meatball. Place the meatballs in Multi-Purpose Tin or 20cm cake tin. Then transfer the tin to the tray.
4. Close the lid and flip the SmartSwitch to RAPID COOKER. Select STEAM AIR FRY, set temperature to 180°C, and set time to 15 minutes. Press START/STOP to begin cooking (the unit will steam for approx. 4 minutes, before countdown time begins).
5. With 5 minutes remaining, open the lid and top with the tomato sauce and pasta sauce.
6. Serve hot.

Italian Sausage Meatballs

Prep: 15 minutes, Total Cook Time: 14 minutes, Steam: approx. 4 minutes, Cook: 10 minutes, Serves: 4

INGREDIENTS:

- 125 ml water, for steaming
- 100 g sausage, casing removed
- ½ medium onion, minced finely
- 1 tsp. fresh sage, chopped finely
- 20 g Italian breadcrumbs
- ½ tsp. garlic, minced
- Salt and black pepper, to taste

DIRECTIONS:

1. Pour 125 ml water into the pot. Pull out the legs on the Cook & Crisp tray, then place the tray in the top position in the pot.
2. Mix all the ingredients in a bowl until well combined.
3. Shape the mixture into equal-sized balls and arrange the balls on the tray.
4. Close the lid and flip the SmartSwitch to RAPID COOKER. Select STEAM AIR FRY, set temperature to 190°C, and set time to 10 minutes. Press START/STOP to begin cooking (the unit will steam for approx. 4 minutes, before countdown time begins).
5. With 5 minutes remaining, open the lid and flip the meatballs with tongs. Close the lid to continue cooking.
6. When cooking is complete, dish out to serve warm.

Cheddar Turkey Burgers

Prep: 10 minutes, Total Cook Time: 19 minutes, Steam: approx. 4 minutes, Cook: 15 minutes, Serves: 4

INGREDIENTS:

- 250 ml water, for steaming
- 40 g finely crushed tortilla chips
- 1 egg, beaten
- 60 ml salsa
- 30 g shredded Cheddar cheese
- Pinch of salt
- Freshly ground black pepper, to taste
- 450 g minced turkey
- 15 ml olive oil
- 1 tsp. paprika

DIRECTIONS:

1. Pour 250 ml water into the pot. Push in the legs on the Cook & Crisp tray, then place the tray in the bottom position in the pot.
2. In a medium bowl, combine the tortilla chips, egg, salsa, cheese, salt, and pepper, and mix well.
3. Add the turkey and mix gently but thoroughly with clean hands.
4. Form the meat mixture into patties about 1 cm thick. Make an indentation in the centre of each patty with your thumb so the burgers don't puff up while cooking.
5. Brush the patties on both sides with the olive oil and sprinkle with paprika.
6. Put the patties on the tray.
7. Close the lid and flip the SmartSwitch to RAPID COOKER. Select STEAM AIR FRY, set temperature to 180°C, and set time to 15 minutes. Press START/STOP to begin cooking (the unit will steam for approx. 4 minutes, before countdown time begins), until the meat registers at least 75°C.
8. When cooking is complete, let sit for 5 minutes before serving.

Cheddar Turkey Burgers

Prep: 10 minutes, Total Cook Time: 19 minutes, Steam: approx. 4 minutes, Cook: 15 minutes, Serves: 4

INGREDIENTS:

- 250 ml water, for steaming
- 40 g finely crushed tortilla chips
- 1 egg, beaten
- 60 ml salsa
- 30 g shredded Cheddar cheese
- Pinch of salt
- Freshly ground black pepper, to taste
- 450 g minced turkey
- 15 ml olive oil
- 1 tsp. paprika

DIRECTIONS:

1. Pour 250 ml water into the pot. Push in the legs on the Cook & Crisp tray, then place the tray in the bottom position in the pot.
2. In a medium bowl, combine the tortilla chips, egg, salsa, cheese, salt, and pepper, and mix well.
3. Add the turkey and mix gently but thoroughly with clean hands.
4. Form the meat mixture into patties about 1 cm thick. Make an indentation in the centre of each patty with your thumb so the burgers don't puff up while cooking.
5. Brush the patties on both sides with the olive oil and sprinkle with paprika.
6. Put the patties on the tray.
7. Close the lid and flip the SmartSwitch to RAPID COOKER. Select STEAM AIR FRY, set temperature to 180°C, and set time to 15 minutes. Press START/STOP to begin cooking (the unit will steam for approx. 4 minutes, before countdown time begins), until the meat registers at least 75°C.
8. When cooking is complete, let sit for 5 minutes before serving.

Portabella Pizza Treat

Prep: 10 minutes, Total Cook Time: 12 minutes, Steam: approx. 4 minutes, Cook: 8 minutes, Serves: 2

INGREDIENTS:

- 125 ml water, for steaming
- 2 Portabella caps, stemmed
- 30 g tinned tomatoes with basil
- 15 g mozzarella cheese, shredded
- 4 pepperoni slices
- 10 g Parmesan cheese, grated freshly
- 30 ml olive oil
- ⅛ tsp. dried Italian seasonings
- Salt, to taste
- 1 tsp. red pepper flakes, crushed

DIRECTIONS:

1. Pour 125 ml water into the pot. Push in the legs on the Cook & Crisp tray, then place the tray in the bottom position in the pot.
2. Drizzle olive oil on both sides of portabella cap and season salt, red pepper flakes and Italian seasonings.
3. Top canned tomatoes on the mushrooms, followed by mozzarella cheese. Transfer the portabella caps to the tray.
4. Close the lid and flip the SmartSwitch to RAPID COOKER. Select STEAM AIR FRY, set temperature to 200°C, and set time to 8 minutes. Press START/STOP to begin cooking (the unit will steam for approx. 4 minutes, before countdown time begins).
5. With 4 minutes remaining, open the lid and top with pepperoni slices. Close the lid to continue cooking.
6. When cooking is complete, use tongs to remove the portabella caps from the tray.
7. Sprinkle with Parmesan cheese and dish out to serve warm.

Chicken with Pineapple and Peach

Prep: 10 minutes, Total Cook Time: 20 minutes, Steam: approx. 4 minutes, Cook: 16 minutes, Serves: 4

INGREDIENTS:

- 125 ml water, for steaming
- 450 g low-sodium boneless, skinless chicken breasts, cut into 2.5 cm pieces
- 1 medium red onion, chopped
- 1 (225 g) tin of pineapple chunks, drained, 60 ml juice reserved
- 15 ml peanut oil or safflower oil
- 1 peach, peeled, pitted, and cubed
- 1 tbsp. cornflour
- ½ tsp. ground ginger
- ¼ tsp. ground allspice
- Brown rice, cooked (optional)

DIRECTIONS:

1. Pour 125 ml water into the pot. Pull out the legs on the Cook & Crisp tray, then place the tray in the top position in the pot.
2. In a medium metal bowl, mix the chicken, red onion, pineapple, and peanut oil. Transfer the chicken mixture to the tray.
3. Close the lid and flip the SmartSwitch to RAPID COOKER. Select STEAM AIR FRY, set temperature to 200°C, and set time to 16 minutes. Press START/STOP to begin cooking (the unit will steam for approx. 4 minutes, before countdown time begins).
4. With 6 minutes remaining, open the lid and add the peach. Close the lid to continue cooking.
5. Meanwhile, in a small bowl, whisk the reserved pineapple juice, the cornflour, ginger, and allspice well.
6. With 3 minutes remaining, open the lid. Add the sauce to the chicken mixture and stir. Close the lid to continue cooking, until the chicken reaches an internal temperature of 74ºC on a meat thermometer and the sauce is slightly thickened.
7. Serve immediately over hot cooked brown rice, if desired.

Glazed Brussels Sprouts

Prep: 10 minutes, Total Cook Time: 14 minutes, Steam: approx. 4 minutes, Cook: 10 minutes, Serves: 2

INGREDIENTS:

- 125 ml water, for steaming
- 340 g Brussels sprouts, trimmed and halved lengthwise
- 15 ml balsamic vinegar
- 15 ml maple syrup
- Salt, as required

DIRECTIONS:

1. Pour 125 ml water into the pot. Push in the legs on the Cook & Crisp tray, then place the tray in the bottom position in the pot.
2. Mix all the ingredients in a bowl and toss to coat well. Arrange the Brussels sprouts on the tray.
3. Close the lid and flip the SmartSwitch to RAPID COOKER. Select STEAM AIR FRY, set temperature to 220°C, and set time to 10 minutes. Press START/STOP to begin cooking (the unit will steam for approx. 4 minutes, before countdown time begins).
4. With 5 minutes remaining, open the lid and toss the Brussels sprouts with tongs. Close the lid to continue cooking.
5. When cooking is complete, use tongs to remove the Brussels sprouts from the tray and serve hot.

CHAPTER 4
STEAM BAKE

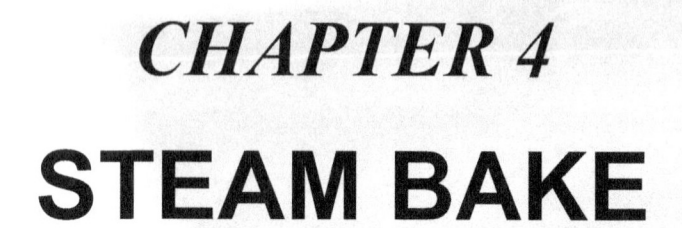

Savory Tuna Cakes

Prep: 20 minutes, Total Cook Time: 20 minutes, Steam: approx. 8 minutes, Cook: 12 minutes, Serves: 4

INGREDIENTS:

- 250 ml water, for steaming
- 1 onion, chopped
- 2 (170 g) tins of tuna, drained
- 1 medium boiled potato, mashed
- 100 g celery
- 130 g breadcrumbs
- 2 eggs
- 7 ml olive oil
- 1 tbsp. fresh ginger, grated
- Salt, as required

DIRECTIONS:

1. Pour 250 ml water into the pot. Push in the legs on the Cook & Crisp tray, then place the tray in the bottom position in the pot.
2. Heat olive oil in a frying pan and add onions, ginger, and green chili.
3. Sauté for about 30 seconds and add the tuna.
4. Stir fry for about 3 minutes and dish out the tuna mixture onto a large bowl.
5. Add mashed potato, celery, and salt and mix well.
6. Make 4 equal-sized patties from the mixture.
7. Place the breadcrumbs in a shallow bowl and whisk the egg in another bowl.
8. Dredge each patty with breadcrumbs, then dip into egg and coat again with the breadcrumbs. Arrange tuna cakes on the tray.
9. Close the lid and flip the SmartSwitch to RAPID COOKER. Select STEAM BAKE, set temperature to 200°C, and set time to 8 minutes. Press START/STOP to begin cooking (the unit will steam for approx. 8 minutes, before countdown time begins).
10. With 4 minutes remaining, open the lid and flip the side with tongs. Close the lid to continue cooking.
11. Dish out the tuna cakes onto serving plates and serve warm.

Mushroom and Bell Pepper Pizza

Prep: 10 minutes, Total Cook Time: 30 minutes, Steam: approx. 20 minutes, Cook: 10 minutes, Serves: 6

INGREDIENTS:

- 250 ml water, for steaming
- cooking spray
- 1 pizza dough, cut into squares
- 150 g chopped oyster mushrooms
- 1 shallot, chopped
- ¼ red bell pepper, chopped
- 2 tbsps. parsley
- Salt and ground black pepper, to taste

DIRECTIONS:

1. Pour 250 ml water into the pot. Push in the legs on the Cook & Crisp tray, then place the tray in the bottom position in the pot. Spray Multi-Purpose Tin or 20cm cake tin with cooking spray.
2. In a bowl, combine the oyster mushrooms, shallot, bell pepper and parsley. Sprinkle some salt and pepper as desired.
3. Spread this mixture on top of the pizza squares.
4. Transfer the pizza squares to the prepared tin, then place the tin on the tray.
5. Close the lid and flip the SmartSwitch to RAPID COOKER. Select STEAM BAKE, set temperature to 175°C, and set time to 10 minutes. Press START/STOP to begin cooking (the unit will steam for approx. 20 minutes, before countdown time begins).
6. When cooking is complete, serve warm.

Honey Pumpkin Bread

Prep: 10 minutes, Total Cook Time: 35 minutes, Steam: approx. 20 minutes, Cook: 15 minutes, Serves: 4

INGREDIENTS:

- 250 ml water, for steaming
- cooking spray
- 2 large eggs
- 40 g coconut flour
- 60 ml plain Greek yogurt
- 60 ml honey
- 8 tbsps. pumpkin puree
- 6 tbsps. oats
- 2 tbsps. vanilla extract
- Pinch of ground nutmeg

DIRECTIONS:

1. Pour 250 ml water into the pot. Push in the legs on the Cook & Crisp tray, then place the tray in the bottom position in the pot. Spray a loaf tin with cooking spray.
2. Mix together all the ingredients except oats in a bowl and beat with the hand mixer until smooth. Add oats and mix until well combined.
3. Transfer the mixture into the prepared loaf tin and place the tin on the tray.
4. Close the lid and flip the SmartSwitch to RAPID COOKER. Select STEAM BAKE, set temperature to 180°C, and set time to 15 minutes. Press START/STOP to begin cooking (the unit will steam for approx. 20 minutes, before countdown time begins).
5. When cooking is complete, transfer onto a wire rack to cool and cut the bread into desired size slices to serve.

Bacon and Spinach Cups

Prep: 15 minutes, Total Cook Time: 35 minutes, Steam: approx. 20 minutes, Cook: 15 minutes, Serves: 4

INGREDIENTS:

- 250 ml water, for steaming
- cooking spray
- 6 large eggs
- 75 g red peppers, chopped
- 25 g fresh spinach, chopped
- 75 g mozzarella cheese, shredded
- 4 rashers of bacon, cooked and crumbled
- 30 ml double cream
- Salt and black pepper, to taste

DIRECTIONS:

1. Pour 250 ml water into the pot. Push in the legs on the Cook & Crisp tray, then place the tray in the bottom position in the pot. Spray 4 silicone molds with cooking spray.
2. Whisk together eggs with cream, salt and black pepper in a large bowl until combined.
3. Stir in rest of the ingredients and transfer the mixture into silicone molds, then place the silicone molds on the tray.
4. Close the lid and flip the SmartSwitch to RAPID COOKER. Select STEAM BAKE, set temperature to 180°C, and set time to 15 minutes. Press START/STOP to begin cooking (the unit will steam for approx. 20 minutes, before countdown time begins).
5. Dish out and serve warm.

Beef and Spinach Rolls

Prep: 10 minutes, Total Cook Time: 22 minutes, Steam: approx. 4 minutes, Cook: 18 minutes, Serves: 2

INGREDIENTS:

- 250 ml water, for steaming
- 900 g beef flank steak
- 3 tsps. pesto
- 6 slices mozzarella cheese
- 85 g roasted red bell peppers
- 45 g baby spinach
- 1 tsp. sea salt
- 1 tsp. black pepper

DIRECTIONS:

1. Pour 250 ml water into the pot. Push in the legs on the Cook & Crisp tray, then place the tray in the bottom position in the pot.
2. Scoop equal amounts of the pesto onto each flank steak and spread it across evenly.
3. Place the cheese, roasted red peppers and spinach on top of the meat, about three-quarters of the way down.
4. Roll the steak up, holding it in place with toothpicks. Season with the sea salt and pepper. Put the Roll on the tray.
5. Close the lid and flip the SmartSwitch to RAPID COOKER. Select STEAM BAKE, set temperature to 190°C, and set time to 18 minutes. Press START/STOP to begin cooking (the unit will steam for approx. 4 minutes, before countdown time begins).
6. Let rest for 10 minutes before slicing up and serving.

Icing Strawberry Cupcakes

Prep: 10 minutes, Total Cook Time: 18 minutes, Steam: approx. 10 minutes, Cook: 8 minutes, Serves: 8

INGREDIENTS:

- 250 ml water, for steaming
- cooking spray

For the Cupcakes:
- 100 unsalted butter
- 2 medium eggs
- 175 g self-raising flour
- 100 g caster sugar
- ½ tsp. vanilla extract

For the Icing:
- 50 g unsalted butter
- 60 ml blended fresh strawberries
- 120 g icing sugar
- 1 tbsp. whipped cream
- ½ tsp. pink food colouring

DIRECTIONS:

1. Pour 250 ml water into the pot. Push in the legs on the Cook & Crisp tray, then place the tray in the bottom position in the pot. Spray 8 muffin tins with cooking spray.
2. Mix all the ingredients for the cupcakes in a large bowl until well combined.
3. Transfer the mixture into muffin tins and place on the tray.
4. Close the lid and flip the SmartSwitch to RAPID COOKER. Select STEAM BAKE, set temperature to 180°C, and set time to 8 minutes. Press START/STOP to begin cooking (the unit will steam for approx. 10 minutes, before countdown time begins).
5. Mix all the ingredients for icing in a large bowl until well combined.
6. Fill the pastry bag with icing and top each cupcake evenly with frosting to serve.

Parmesan Sausage Muffins

Prep: 5 minutes, Total Cook Time: 35 minutes, Steam: approx. 20 minutes, Cook: 15 minutes, Serves: 4

INGREDIENTS:

- 250 ml water, for steaming
- cooking spray
- 170 g Italian sausage, sliced
- 6 eggs
- 30 ml double cream
- Salt and ground black pepper, to taste
- 85 g Parmesan cheese, grated

DIRECTIONS:

1. Pour 250 ml water into the pot. Push in the legs on the Cook & Crisp tray, then place the tray in the bottom position in the pot. Spray a muffin tin with cooking spray.
2. Put the sliced sausage in the muffin tin. Beat the eggs with the cream in a bowl and season with salt and pepper. Pour half of the mixture over the sausages in the tin. Sprinkle with cheese and the remaining egg mixture. Then place the tin on the tray.
3. Close the lid and flip the SmartSwitch to RAPID COOKER. Select STEAM BAKE, set temperature to 180°C, and set time to 15 minutes. Press START/STOP to begin cooking (the unit will steam for approx. 20 minutes, before count-down time begins).
4. When cooking is complete, serve immediately.

Peanut Butter Banana Bread

Prep: 15 minutes, Total Cook Time: 45 minutes, Steam: approx. 25 minutes, Cook: 20 minutes, Serves: 6

INGREDIENTS:

- 750 ml water, for steaming
- cooking spray
- 190 g plain flour
- 1¼ tsps. baking powder
- 1 large egg
- 2 medium ripe bananas, peeled and mashed
- 75 g walnuts, roughly chopped
- ¼ tsp. salt
- 75 g granulated sugar
- 60 ml rapeseed oil
- 2 tbsps. creamy peanut butter
- 30 ml sour cream
- 1 tsp. vanilla extract

DIRECTIONS:

1. Pour 750 ml water into the pot. Push in the legs on the Cook & Crisp tray, then place the tray in the bottom position in the pot. Spray Multi-Purpose Tin or 20cm cake tin with cooking spray.
2. Mix together the flour, baking powder and salt in a bowl.
3. Whisk together egg with sugar, rapeseed oil, sour cream, peanut butter and vanilla extract in a bowl.
4. Stir in the bananas and beat until well combined.
5. Now, add the flour mixture and fold in the walnuts gently.
6. Mix until combined and transfer the mixture evenly into the prepared tin, then place the tin on the tray.
7. Close the lid and flip the SmartSwitch to RAPID COOKER. Select STEAM BAKE, set temperature to 175°C, and set time to 20 minutes. Press START/STOP to begin cooking (the unit will steam for approx. 25 minutes, before count-down time begins).
8. When cooking is complete, carefully remove the tin and place onto a wire rack to cool.
9. Cut the bread into desired size slices and serve.

Nutty Courgette Bread

Prep: 15 minutes, Total Cook Time: 45 minutes, Steam: approx. 25 minutes, Cook: 20 minutes, Serves: 6

INGREDIENTS:

- 750 ml water, for steaming
- cooking spray
- 375 g plain flour
- 2 tsp. baking powder
- 3 eggs
- 300 g courgette, grated
- 150 g walnuts, chopped
- 1 tbsp. ground cinnamon
- 1 tsp. Salt
- 450 g caster sugar
- 240 ml vegetable oil
- 3 tsp. vanilla extract

DIRECTIONS:

1. Pour 750 ml water into the pot. Push in the legs on the Cook & Crisp tray, then place the tray in the bottom position in the pot. Spray two (20x10 cm) loaf tins with cooking spray.
2. Mix together the flour, baking powder, cinnamon and salt in a bowl
3. Whisk together eggs with sugar, vanilla extract and vegetable oil in a bowl until combined.
4. Stir in the flour mixture and fold in the courgette and walnuts.
5. Mix until combined and transfer the mixture into the prepared loaf tins.
6. Arrange the loaf tins on the tray.
7. Close the lid and flip the SmartSwitch to RAPID COOKER. Select STEAM BAKE, set temperature to 160°C, and set time to 20 minutes. Press START/STOP to begin cooking (the unit will steam for approx. 25 minutes, before countdown time begins).
8. When cooking is complete, remove from the tray and place onto a wire rack to cool.
9. Cut the bread into desired size slices and serve.

Prawn Burgers

Prep: 20 minutes, Total Cook Time: 10 minutes, Steam: approx. 4 minutes, Cook: 6 minutes, Serves: 2

INGREDIENTS:

- 250 ml water, for steaming
- 75 g prawns, peeled, deveined and finely chopped
- 60 g breadcrumbs
- 2-3 tbsps. onion, finely chopped
- 75 g fresh baby greens
- ½ tsp. ginger, minced
- ½ tsp. garlic, minced
- ½ tsp. spices powder
- ½ tsp. ground cumin
- ¼ tsp. ground turmeric
- Salt and ground black pepper, as required

DIRECTIONS:

1. Pour 250 ml water into the pot. Push in the legs on the Cook & Crisp tray, then place the tray in the bottom position in the pot.
2. Mix the prawns, breadcrumbs, onion, ginger, garlic, and spices in a bowl.
3. Make small-sized patties from the mixture and transfer on the tray.
4. Close the lid and flip the SmartSwitch to RAPID COOKER. Select STEAM BAKE, set temperature to 200°C, and set time to 6 minutes. Press START/STOP to begin cooking (the unit will steam for approx. 4 minutes, before countdown time begins).
5. When cooking is complete, dish out in a platter.
6. Serve immediately warm alongside the baby greens.

Creamy Cheese Soufflé

Prep: 5 minutes, Total Cook Time: 30 minutes, Steam: approx. 20 minutes, Cook: 10 minutes, Serves: 2

INGREDIENTS:

- 250 ml water, for steaming
- cooking spray
- 2 eggs
- 1 tbsp. fresh parsley, chopped
- 1 fresh red chili pepper, chopped
- 30 ml single cream
- Salt, to taste

DIRECTIONS:

1. Pour 250 ml water into the pot. Push in the legs on the Cook & Crisp tray, then place the tray in the bottom position in the pot. Spray 2 soufflé dishes with cooking spray.
2. Mix together all the ingredients in a bowl until well combined.
3. Transfer the mixture into prepared soufflé dishes and place on the tray.
4. Close the lid and flip the SmartSwitch to RAPID COOKER. Select STEAM BAKE, set temperature to 180°C, and set time to 10 minutes. Press START/STOP to begin cooking (the unit will steam for approx. 20 minutes, before countdown time begins).
5. When cooking is complete, dish out to serve warm.

Eggless Spinach and Bacon Quiche

Prep: 15 minutes, Total Cook Time: 30 minutes, Steam: approx. 20 minutes, Cook: 10 minutes, Serves: 2

INGREDIENTS:

- 250 ml water, for steaming
- cooking spray
- 100 g fresh spinach, chopped
- 4 rashers of bacon, cooked and chopped
- 50 g mozzarella cheese, shredded
- 60 ml milk
- 80 g Parmesan cheese, shredded
- 4 dashes Tabasco sauce
- Salt and black pepper, to taste

DIRECTIONS:

1. Pour 250 ml water into the pot. Push in the legs on the Cook & Crisp tray, then place the tray in the bottom position in the pot. Spray Multi-Purpose Tin or 20cm cake tin with cooking spray.
2. Mix together all the ingredients in a bowl and transfer the mixture into the prepared tin, then place the tin on the tray.
3. Close the lid and flip the SmartSwitch to RAPID COOKER. Select STEAM BAKE, set temperature to 165°C, and set time to 10 minutes. Press START/STOP to begin cooking (the unit will steam for approx. 20 minutes, before countdown time begins).
4. Dish out and serve warm.

Vanilla Pecan Pie

Prep: 10 minutes, Total Cook Time: 50 minutes, Steam: approx. 20 minutes, Cook: 30 minutes, Serves: 6

INGREDIENTS:

- 250 ml water, for steaming
- cooking spray
- 75 g butter, melted
- 2 large eggs
- 20 g plain flour
- 100 g pecan halves
- 1 frozen pie crust, thawed
- 75 g brown sugar
- 50 g caster sugar
- 1 tsp. vanilla extract

DIRECTIONS:

1. Pour 250 ml water into the pot. Push in the legs on the Cook & Crisp tray, then place the tray in the bottom position in the pot. Spray a pie pan with cooking spray.
2. Mix both sugars, eggs and butter in a bowl until smooth.
3. Stir in the flour, milk and vanilla extract and beat until well combined.
4. Fold in the pecan halves and arrange the crust in the bottom of pie pan.
5. Put the pecan mixture in pie crust evenly and transfer on the tray.
6. Close the lid and flip the SmartSwitch to RAPID COOKER. Select STEAM BAKE, set temperature to 160°C, and set time to 30 minutes. Press START/STOP to begin cooking (the unit will steam for approx. 20 minutes, before countdown time begins).
7. With 10 minutes remaining, reduce the temperature to 150ºC. Continue cooking until the pie is golden down.
8. Dish out to serve hot.

Walnut Chocolate Cake

Prep: 10 minutes, Total Cook Time: 50 minutes, Steam: approx. 20 minutes, Cook: 30 minutes, Serves: 4

INGREDIENTS:

- 750 ml water, for steaming
- Unsalted butter, at room temperature
- 3 large eggs
- 120 g almond flour
- 150 g sugar
- 80 ml double cream
- 25 g chopped walnuts
- 60 ml coconut oil, melted
- 25 g unsweetened cocoa powder
- 1 tsp. baking powder

DIRECTIONS:

1. Pour 750 ml water into the pot. Push in the legs on the Cook & Crisp tray, then place the tray in the bottom position in the pot. Generously butter Multi-Purpose Tin or 20cm cake tin. Line the bottom of the tin with parchment paper cut to fit.
2. In a large bowl, mix the eggs, almond flour, cream, sugar, coconut oil, cocoa powder, and baking powder. Beat with a hand mixer on medium speed until well blended and fluffy. Gently fold in the walnuts.
3. Pour the batter into the prepared tin and transfer the tin on the tray.
4. Close the lid and flip the SmartSwitch to RAPID COOKER. Select STEAM BAKE, set temperature to 200°C, and set time to 30 minutes. Press START/STOP to begin cooking (the unit will steam for approx. 20 minutes, before countdown time begins), until a knife (do not use a toothpick) inserted into the centre of the cake comes out clean.
5. Let the cake cool in the tin on a wire rack for 30 minutes before slicing and serving.

Chocolate Cherry Turnovers

Prep: 10 minutes, Total Cook Time: 30 minutes, Steam: approx. 15 minutes, Cook: 15 minutes, Serves: 6

INGREDIENTS:

- 250 ml water, for steaming
- cooking spray
- 35 g milk or dark chocolate chips
- 30 ml thick, hot fudge sauce
- 20 g chopped dried cherries
- 1 (25-by-37-cm) sheet frozen puff pastry, thawed
- 1 egg white, beaten
- 25 g coconut sugar
- ½ tsp. cinnamon

DIRECTIONS:

1. Pour 250 ml water into the pot. Push in the legs on the Cook & Crisp tray, then place the tray in the bottom position in the pot. Spray the tray with cooking spray.
2. In a small bowl, combine the chocolate chips, fudge sauce, and dried cherries.
3. Roll out the puff pastry on a floured surface. Cut into 6 squares with a sharp knife.
4. Divide the chocolate chip mixture into the centre of each puff pastry square. Fold the squares in half to make triangles. Firmly press the edges with the tines of a fork to seal.
5. Brush the triangles on all sides sparingly with the beaten egg white. Sprinkle the tops with sugar and cinnamon. Transfer the triangles on the tray.
6. Close the lid and flip the SmartSwitch to RAPID COOKER. Select STEAM BAKE, set temperature to 180°C, and set time to 15 minutes. Press START/STOP to begin cooking (the unit will steam for approx. 15 minutes, before countdown time begins).
7. When cooking is complete, allow to cool for at least 20 minutes before serving.

CHAPTER 5
AIR FRY

Raspberry Wontons

Prep Time: 15 minutes, Cook Time: 8 minutes, Serves: 12

INGREDIENTS:

For the Wonton Wrappers:
- cooking spray
- 500 g cream cheese, softened
- 1 Package of wonton wrappers
- 65 g icing sugar
- 1 tsp. vanilla extract

For the Raspberry Syrup:
- 340 g frozen raspberries
- 60 ml water
- 50 g sugar
- 1 tsp. vanilla extract

DIRECTIONS:

For the Wonton Wrappers:
1. Push in the legs on the Cook & Crisp tray, then place the tray in the bottom of the pot. Spray the tray with cooking spray.
2. Mix sugar, cream cheese and vanilla extract in a bowl and place a wonton wrapper on a work surface. Place about 1 tbsp. of the cream cheese mixture in the centre of each wonton wrapper. Fold the wrappers around the filling and seal the edges.
3. Close the lid and flip the SmartSwitch to AIR FRY/HOB. Select AIRFRY, set temperature to 180°C, and set time to 13 minutes (unit will need to preheat for 5 minutes, so set an external timer if desired). Press START/STOP to begin cooking.
4. When the unit is preheated and the time reaches 8 minutes, place the wontons on the tray. Close the lid to begin cooking.

For the Raspberry Syrup:

5. Put water, sugar, raspberries and vanilla in a skillet on medium heat and cook for about 5 minutes, stirring continuously.
6. Transfer the mixture into the food processor and blend until smooth.
7. Drizzle the raspberry syrup over the wontons to serve.

Breaded Flounder with Lemon

Prep Time: 15 minutes, Cook Time: 12 minutes, Serves: 3

INGREDIENTS:

- cooking spray
- 1 egg
- 80 g dry breadcrumbs
- 3 (170 g each) flounder fillets
- 1 lemon, sliced
- 60 ml vegetable oil

DIRECTIONS:

1. Push in the legs on the Cook & Crisp tray, then place the tray in the bottom of the pot. Spray the tray with cooking spray.
2. Whisk the egg in a shallow bowl and mix breadcrumbs and oil in another bowl.
3. Dip flounder fillets into the whisked egg and coat with the breadcrumb mixture.
4. Close the lid and flip the SmartSwitch to AIR FRY/HOB. Select AIRFRY, set temperature to 200°C, and set time to 17 minutes (unit will need to preheat for 5 minutes, so set an external timer if desired). Press START/STOP to begin cooking.
5. When the unit is preheated and the time reaches 12 minutes, place the flounder fillets on the tray. Close the lid to begin cooking.
6. After 6 minutes, open the lid and flip the flounder fillets with silicone-tipped tongs to ensure even cooking. Close the lid to continue cooking.
7. Dish out the flounder fillets onto serving plates and garnish with the lemon slices to serve.

Jerk Chicken Leg Quarters

Prep: 8 minutes, Total Cook Time: 30 minutes, Serves: 2

INGREDIENTS:

- cooking spray
- 2 (285-g) chicken leg quarters, trimmed
- 5 ml vegetable oil
- 1 tbsp. packed brown sugar
- 1 scallion, green part only, sliced thin
- 1 tsp. ground allspice
- 1 tsp. pepper
- 1 tsp. garlic powder
- ¾ tsp. dry mustard
- ¾ tsp. dried thyme
- ½ tsp. salt
- ¼ tsp. cayenne pepper
- Lime wedges

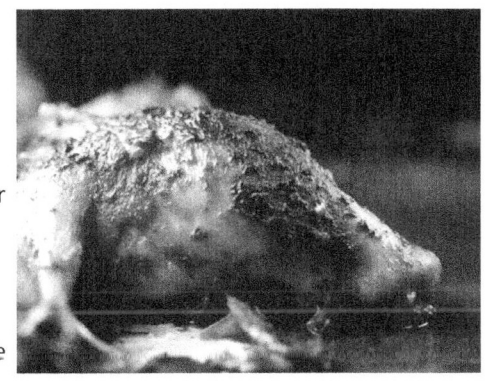

DIRECTIONS:

1. Push in the legs on the Cook & Crisp tray, then place the tray in the bottom of the pot. Spray the tray with cooking spray.
2. Mix sugar, allspice, pepper, garlic powder, mustard, thyme, salt, and cayenne in a bowl. Pat the chicken dry with paper towels. With metal skewer, poke 10 to 15 holes in skin of each chicken leg. Rub with oil and season evenly with spice mixture.
3. Close the lid and flip the SmartSwitch to AIR FRY/HOB. Select AIRFRY, set temperature to 200°C, and set time to 35 minutes (unit will need to preheat for 5 minutes, so set an external timer if desired). Press START/STOP to begin cooking.
4. When the unit is preheated and the time reaches 30 minutes, place the chicken skin-side up on the tray. Close the lid to begin cooking.
5. After 15 minutes, open the lid and rotate the chicken with silicone-tipped tongs to ensure even cooking. Close the lid to continue cooking.
6. When cooking is complete, transfer chicken to plate, tent loosely with aluminium foil, and allow to cool for 5 minutes. Scatter with scallion. Serve hot with lime wedges.

Herbed Radishes

Prep: 5 minutes, Total Cook Time: 10 minutes, Serves: 2

INGREDIENTS:

- cooking spray
- 450 g radishes
- 28 g unsalted butter, melted
- ½ tsp. dried parsley
- ½ tsp. garlic powder
- ¼ tsp. dried oregano

DIRECTIONS:

1. Push in the legs on the Cook & Crisp tray, then place the tray in the bottom of the pot. Spray the tray with cooking spray.
2. Prepare the radishes by cutting off their tops and bottoms and quartering them.
3. In a bowl, mix the butter, dried oregano, dried parsley, and garlic powder. Toss with the radishes to coat well.
4. Close the lid and flip the SmartSwitch to AIR FRY/HOB. Select AIRFRY, set temperature to 200°C, and set time to 15 minutes (unit will need to preheat for 5 minutes, so set an external timer if desired). Press START/STOP to begin cooking.
5. When the unit is preheated and the time reaches 10 minutes, place the radishes on the tray. Close the lid to begin cooking.
6. After 5 minutes, open the lid and toss the radishes with silicone-tipped tongs to ensure even cooking. Close the lid to continue cooking.
7. The radishes are ready when they turn brown.
8. Serve hot.

Beef Steak Fingers

Prep Time: 5 minutes, Cook Time: 8 minutes, Serves: 4

INGREDIENTS:

- 4 small beef cube steaks
- Salt and ground black pepper, to taste
- 60 g whole wheat flour
- Cooking spray

DIRECTIONS:

1. Push in the legs on the Cook & Crisp tray, then place the tray in the bottom of the pot. Spray the tray with cooking spray.
2. Cut cube steaks into 2.5-cm-wide strips. Sprinkle lightly with salt and pepper to taste. Roll in flour to coat all sides.
3. Close the lid and flip the SmartSwitch to AIR FRY/HOB. Select AIRFRY, set temperature to 200°C, and set time to 13 minutes (unit will need to preheat for 5 minutes, so set an external timer if desired). Press START/STOP to begin cooking.
4. When the unit is preheated and the time reaches 8 minutes, place the steak strips on the tray in a single layer. Spritz top of steak strips with cooking spray. Close the lid to begin cooking.
5. After 4 minutes, open the lid. Turn strips over and spritz with cooking spray. Close the lid to continue cooking.
6. Serve immediately.

Buttermilk Paprika Chicken

Prep: 7 minutes, Total Cook Time: 22 minutes, Serves: 4

INGREDIENTS:

- cooking spray
- 4 (140-g) low-sodium boneless, skinless chicken breasts, pounded to about 1 cm thick
- 120 ml buttermilk
- 60 g plain flour
- 1 egg white
- 2 tbsps. cornflour
- 1 tsp. dried thyme
- 1 tsp. ground paprika
- 15 ml olive oil

DIRECTIONS:

1. Push in the legs on the Cook & Crisp tray, then place the tray in the bottom of the pot. Spray the tray with cooking spray.
2. In a shallow bowl, combine the chicken and buttermilk. Allow to stand for 10 minutes.
3. Meanwhile, in another shallow bowl, combine the flour, cornflour, thyme, and paprika.
4. Whisk the egg white and olive oil in a small bowl. Quickly stir this egg mixture into the flour mixture so the dry ingredients are evenly moistened.
5. Transfer the chicken from the buttermilk and shake off any excess liquid. Dunk each piece of chicken into the flour mixture to coat evenly.
6. Close the lid and flip the SmartSwitch to AIR FRY/HOB. Select AIRFRY, set temperature to 190°C, and set time to 27 minutes (unit will need to preheat for 5 minutes, so set an external timer if desired). Press START/STOP to begin cooking.
7. When the unit is preheated and the time reaches 22 minutes, place the chicken on the tray. Close the lid to begin cooking, until the chicken reaches an internal temperature of 74ºC on a meat thermometer.
8. Serve hot.

Easy Crispy Prawns

Prep Time: 15 minutes, Cook Time: 10 minutes, Serves: 4

INGREDIENTS:
- cooking spray
- 1 egg
- 225 g nacho chips, crushed
- 18 large raw prawns, peeled and deveined
- Salt and black pepper, to taste

DIRECTIONS:
1. Push in the legs on the Cook & Crisp tray, then place the tray in the bottom of the pot. Spray the tray with cooking spray.
2. Crack egg in a shallow dish and beat well.
3. Place the crushed nacho chips in another shallow dish.
4. Coat prawns with egg, salt and black pepper, then roll into nacho chips.
5. Close the lid and flip the SmartSwitch to AIR FRY/HOB. Select AIRFRY, set temperature to 200°C, and set time to 15 minutes (unit will need to preheat for 5 minutes, so set an external timer if desired). Press START/STOP to begin cooking.
6. When the unit is preheated and the time reaches 10 minutes, place the coated prawns on the tray. Close the lid to begin cooking.
7. After 5 minutes, open the lid and toss the coated prawns with silicone-tipped tongs to ensure even cooking. Close the lid to continue cooking.
8. When cooking is complete, serve hot.

Air Fried Baby Back Ribs

Prep: 5 minutes, Total Cook Time: 25 minutes, Serves: 2

INGREDIENTS:
- cooking spray
- 2 tsps. red pepper flakes
- ¾ ground ginger
- 3 cloves minced garlic
- Salt and ground black pepper, to taste
- 2 baby back ribs

DIRECTIONS:
1. Push in the legs on the Cook & Crisp tray, then place the tray in the bottom of the pot. Spray the tray with cooking spray.
2. Mix the red pepper flakes, garlic, ginger, salt and pepper in a bowl, making sure to mix well. Massage the mixture into the baby back ribs.
3. Close the lid and flip the SmartSwitch to AIR FRY/HOB. Select AIRFRY, set temperature to 180°C, and set time to 30 minutes (unit will need to preheat for 5 minutes, so set an external timer if desired). Press START/STOP to begin cooking.
4. When the unit is preheated and the time reaches 25 minutes, place the ribs on the tray. Close the lid to begin cooking.
5. When cooking is complete, carefully transfer the ribs to a serving dish and serve hot.

Potato and Bacon Nuggets

Prep Time: 5 minutes, Cook Time: 17 minutes, Serves: 4

INGREDIENTS:

- cooking spray
- 24 frozen potato nuggets
- 6 rashers of cooked bacon
- 30 ml maple syrup
- 100 g grated Cheddar cheese

DIRECTIONS:

1. Push in the legs on the Cook & Crisp tray, then place the tray in the bottom of the pot. Spray the tray with cooking spray.
2. Close the lid and flip the SmartSwitch to AIR FRY/HOB. Select AIRFRY, set temperature to 200°C, and set time to 22 minutes (unit will need to preheat for 5 minutes, so set an external timer if desired). Press START/STOP to begin cooking.
3. When the unit is preheated and the time reaches 17 minutes, place the potato nuggets on the tray. Close the lid to begin cooking. Meanwhile, cut the bacon into 2.5 cm pieces.
4. After 10 minutes, open the lid and flip the potato nuggets with silicone-tipped tongs to ensure even cooking. Top with the bacon and drizzle with the maple syrup. Close the lid to continue cooking.
5. With 2 minutes remaining, open the lid and top with the cheese. Close the lid to continue cooking, until the cheese is melted.
6. Serve hot.

Herbed Beef

Prep: 5 minutes, Total Cook Time: 20 minutes, Serves: 6

INGREDIENTS:

- 900 g beef steak
- 45 g butter
- 1 tsp. dried dill
- 1 tsp. dried thyme
- 1 tsp. garlic powder

DIRECTIONS:

1. Push in the legs on the Cook & Crisp tray, then place the tray in the bottom of the pot.
2. Combine the dill, thyme, and garlic powder in a small bowl, and massage into the steak.
3. Close the lid and flip the SmartSwitch to AIR FRY/HOB. Select AIRFRY, set temperature to 200°C, and set time to 23 minutes (unit will need to preheat for 5 minutes, so set an external timer if desired). Press START/STOP to begin cooking.
4. When the unit is preheated and the time reaches 18 minutes, place the steak on the tray. Close the lid to begin cooking.
5. Then remove, shred, and return to the pot. Add the butter and place the steak on the tray. Air fry for another 2 minutes at 180°C.
6. Serve hot.

Almond-Crusted Chicken Nuggets

Prep: 10 minutes, Total Cook Time: 12 minutes, Serves: 4

INGREDIENTS:

- 1 egg white
- 15 ml freshly squeezed lemon juice
- ½ tsp. dried basil
- ½ tsp. ground paprika
- 450 g low-sodium boneless, skinless chicken breasts, cut into 4-cm cubes
- 60 g ground almonds
- 2 slices low-sodium whole-wheat bread, crumbled

DIRECTIONS:

1. Push in the legs on the Cook & Crisp tray, then place the tray in the bottom of the pot. Spray the tray with cooking spray.
2. In a shallow bowl, beat the egg white, basil, lemon juice, and paprika with a fork until foamy.
3. Add the chicken and stir to coat well. On a plate, combine the almonds and bread crumbs.
4. Toss the chicken cubes in the almond and bread crumb mixture until coated evenly.
5. Close the lid and flip the SmartSwitch to AIR FRY/HOB. Select AIRFRY, set temperature to 200°C, and set time to 17 minutes (unit will need to preheat for 5 minutes, so set an external timer if desired). Press START/STOP to begin cooking.
6. When the unit is preheated and the time reaches 12 minutes, place the nuggets on the tray, working in batches. Close the lid to begin cooking.
7. After 6 minutes, open the lid and flip the nuggets over with silicone-tipped tongs to ensure even cooking. Close the lid to continue cooking, until the chicken reaches an internal temperature of 74°C on a meat thermometer.
8. Serve hot.

Apple Dumplings with Sultana

Prep Time: 10 minutes, Cook Time: 15 minutes, Serves: 2

INGREDIENTS:

- cooking spray
- 2 sheets puff pastry
- 2 small apples, peeled and cored
- 20 g sultanas
- 30 g butter, melted
- 15 g brown sugar

DIRECTIONS:

1. Push in the legs on the Cook & Crisp tray, then place the tray in the bottom of the pot. Spray the tray with cooking spray.
2. Mix sugar and sultanas in a bowl and fill each apple core with it.
3. Place the apple in the centre of each pastry sheet and fold to completely cover the apple. Seal the edges.
4. Close the lid and flip the SmartSwitch to AIR FRY/HOB. Select AIRFRY, set temperature to 200°C, and set time to 20 minutes (unit will need to preheat for 5 minutes, so set an external timer if desired). Press START/STOP to begin cooking.
5. When the unit is preheated and the time reaches 15 minutes, place the dumplings on the tray. Close the lid to begin cooking.
6. After 8 minutes, open the lid and toss the dumplings with silicone-tipped tongs to ensure even cooking. Close the lid to continue cooking.
7. When cooking is complete, serve hot.

Crispy Artichoke Hearts

Prep Time: 5 minutes, Cook Time: 8 minutes, Serves: 14

INGREDIENTS:

- 14 whole artichoke hearts, packed in water
- 1 egg
- 60 g plain flour
- 30 g panko bread crumbs
- 1 tsp. Italian seasoning
- Cooking spray

DIRECTIONS:

1. Push in the legs on the Cook & Crisp tray, then place the tray in the bottom of the pot. Spray the tray with cooking spray.
2. Squeeze excess water from the artichoke hearts and place them on paper towels to dry.
3. In a small bowl, beat the egg. In another small bowl, place the flour. In a third small bowl, combine the bread crumbs and Italian seasoning, and stir.
4. Dip the artichoke hearts in the flour, then the egg, and then the bread crumb mixture.
5. Close the lid and flip the SmartSwitch to AIR FRY/HOB. Select AIRFRY, set temperature to 200°C, and set time to 13 minutes (unit will need to preheat for 5 minutes, so set an external timer if desired). Press START/STOP to begin cooking.
6. When the unit is preheated and the time reaches 8 minutes, place the breaded artichoke hearts on the tray. Close the lid to begin cooking.
7. After 4 minutes, open the lid and flip the artichoke hearts with silicone-tipped tongs to ensure even cooking. Close the lid to continue cooking, until the artichoke hearts have browned and are crisp.
8. Let cool for 5 minutes before serving.

Air Fried Chicken Tenders

Prep Time: 15 minutes, Cook Time: 18 minutes, Serves: 4

INGREDIENTS:

- cooking spray
- 340 g chicken breasts, cut into tenders
- 1 egg white
- 20 g plain flour
- 50 g panko bread crumbs
- Salt and black pepper, to taste

DIRECTIONS:

1. Push in the legs on the Cook & Crisp tray, then place the tray in the bottom of the pot. Spray the tray with cooking spray.
2. Season the chicken tenders with salt and black pepper.
3. Coat the chicken tenders with flour, then dip in egg whites and then dredge in the panko bread crumbs.
4. Close the lid and flip the SmartSwitch to AIR FRY/HOB. Select AIRFRY, set temperature to 190°C, and set time to 23 minutes (unit will need to preheat for 5 minutes, so set an external timer if desired). Press START/STOP to begin cooking.
5. When the unit is preheated and the time reaches 18 minutes, place the chicken tenders on the tray. Close the lid to begin cooking.
6. After 10 minutes, open the lid and toss the chicken tenders with silicone-tipped tongs to ensure even cooking. Close the lid to continue cooking.
7. When the time is up, serve chicken tenders hot.

Chilli Fingerling Potatoes

Prep Time: 10 minutes, Cook Time: 18 minutes, Serves: 4

INGREDIENTS:

- cooking spray
- 450 g fingerling potatoes, rinsed and cut into wedges
- 5 ml olive oil
- 1 tsp. salt
- 1 tsp. black pepper
- 1 tsp. cayenne pepper
- 1 tsp. nutritional yeast
- ½ tsp. garlic powder

DIRECTIONS:

1. Push in the legs on the Cook & Crisp tray, then place the tray in the bottom of the pot. Spray the tray with cooking spray.
2. Coat the potatoes with the rest of the ingredients.
3. Close the lid and flip the SmartSwitch to AIR FRY/HOB. Select AIRFRY, set temperature to 200°C, and set time to 23 minutes (unit will need to preheat for 5 minutes, so set an external timer if desired). Press START/STOP to begin cooking.
4. When the unit is preheated and the time reaches 18 minutes, place the potatoes on the tray. Close the lid to begin cooking.
5. After 10 minutes, open the lid and toss the potatoes with silicone-tipped tongs to ensure even cooking. Close the lid to continue cooking.
6. When cooking is complete, serve hot.

CHAPTER 6
BAKE/ROAST

Balsamic Asparagus with Almond

Prep Time: 15 minutes, Cook Time: 8 minutes, Serves: 3

INGREDIENTS:

- Cooking spray
- 450 g asparagus
- 40 g sliced almonds
- 30 ml olive oil
- 30 ml balsamic vinegar
- Salt and black pepper, to taste

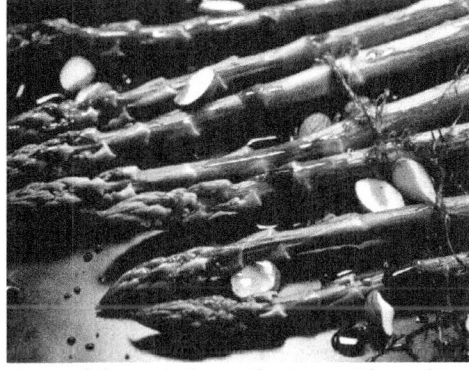

DIRECTIONS:

1. Push in the legs on the Cook & Crisp tray, then place the tray in the bottom of the pot. Spray the tray with cooking spray.
2. Mix asparagus, oil, vinegar, salt, and black pepper in a bowl and toss to coat well.
3. Close the lid and flip the SmartSwitch to AIR FRY/HOB. Select BAKE & ROAST, set temperature to 200°C, and set time to 13 minutes (unit will need to preheat for 5 minutes, so set an external timer if desired). Press START/STOP to begin cooking.
4. When the unit is preheated and the time reaches 8 minutes, place the asparagus on the tray and sprinkle with the almond slices. Close the lid to begin cooking.
5. After 4 minutes, open the lid and toss the asparagus with silicone-tipped tongs to ensure even cooking. Close the lid to continue cooking.
6. When cooking is complete, serve hot.

Roasted Aubergine Slices

Prep Time: 5 minutes, Cook Time: 15 minutes, Serves: 1

INGREDIENTS:

- cooking spray
- 1 large aubergine, sliced
- 30 ml olive oil
- ¼ tsp. Salt
- ½ tsp. garlic powder

DIRECTIONS:

1. Push in the legs on the Cook & Crisp tray, then place the tray in the bottom of the pot. Spray the tray with cooking spray.
2. Apply the olive oil to the aubergine slices with a brush, coating both sides. Season each side with sprinklings of salt and garlic powder.
3. Close the lid and flip the SmartSwitch to AIR FRY/HOB. Select BAKE & ROAST, set temperature to 200°C, and set time to 20 minutes (unit will need to preheat for 5 minutes, so set an external timer if desired). Press START/STOP to begin cooking.
4. When the unit is preheated and the time reaches 15 minutes, place the aubergine slices on the tray. Close the lid to begin cooking.
5. After 8 minutes, open the lid and flip the aubergine slices with silicone-tipped tongs to ensure even cooking. Close the lid to continue cooking.
6. When cooking is complete, serve hot.

Easy Roasted Salmon

Prep Time: 5 minutes, Cook Time: 10 minutes, Serves: 2

INGREDIENTS:

- cooking spray
- 2 (170 g) salmon fillets
- Salt and black pepper, as required
- 15 ml olive oil

DIRECTIONS:

1. Push in the legs on the Cook & Crisp tray, then place the tray in the bottom of the pot. Spray the tray with cooking spray.
2. Season each salmon fillet with salt and black pepper and drizzle with olive oil.
3. Close the lid and flip the SmartSwitch to AIR FRY/HOB. Select BAKE & ROAST, set temperature to 200°C, and set time to 15 minutes (unit will need to preheat for 5 minutes, so set an external timer if desired). Press START/STOP to begin cooking.
4. When the unit is preheated and the time reaches 10 minutes, place the salmon fillets on the tray. Close the lid to begin cooking.
5. After 5 minutes, open the lid and toss the salmon fillets with silicone-tipped tongs to ensure even cooking. Close the lid to continue cooking.
6. Dish out the salmon fillets onto the serving plates.

Crispy Cod Cakes with Salad Greens

Prep: 15 minutes, Total Cook Time: 10 minutes, Serves: 4

INGREDIENTS:

- Cooking spray
- 450 g cod fillets, cut into chunks
- 1 large egg, beaten
- 100 g panko bread crumbs
- 30 g packed fresh basil leaves
- 3 cloves garlic, crushed
- ½ tsp. smoked paprika
- ¼ tsp. salt
- ¼ tsp. pepper
- Salad greens, for serving

DIRECTIONS:

1. Push in the legs on the Cook & Crisp tray, then place the tray in the bottom of the pot. Spray the tray with cooking spray.
2. In a food processor, pulse cod, basil, smoked paprika, garlic, salt, and pepper until cod is finely chopped, stirring occasionally. Shape into 8 patties, about 5 cm in diameter. Dunk each first into the egg, then into the panko, patting to adhere. Spritz with oil on one side.
3. Close the lid and flip the SmartSwitch to AIR FRY/HOB. Select BAKE & ROAST, set temperature to 200°C, and set time to 15 minutes (unit will need to preheat for 5 minutes, so set an external timer if desired). Press START/STOP to begin cooking.
4. When the unit is preheated and the time reaches 10 minutes, place half the cakes on the tray, working in batches. Close the lid to begin cooking.
5. After 5 minutes, open the lid and flip the cakes over with silicone-tipped tongs to ensure even cooking. Close the lid to continue cooking.
6. Serve cod cakes hot with salad greens.

Spiced Turkey Tenderloin

Prep Time: 20 minutes, Cook Time: 30 minutes, Serves: 4

INGREDIENTS:

- ½ tsp. paprika
- ½ tsp. garlic powder
- ½ tsp. salt
- ½ tsp. freshly ground black pepper
- Pinch cayenne pepper
- 680 g turkey breast tenderloin
- Olive oil spray

DIRECTIONS:

1. Push in the legs on the Cook & Crisp tray, then place the tray in the bottom of the pot. Spray the tray with olive oil spray.
2. In a small bowl, combine the paprika, garlic powder, salt, black pepper, and cayenne pepper. Rub the mixture all over the turkey.
3. Close the lid and flip the SmartSwitch to AIR FRY/HOB. Select BAKE & ROAST, set temperature to 190°C, and set time to 35 minutes (unit will need to preheat for 5 minutes, so set an external timer if desired). Press START/STOP to begin cooking.
4. When the unit is preheated and the time reaches 30 minutes, place the turkey on the tray. Lightly spray with olive oil spray. Close the lid to begin cooking.
5. After 15 minutes, open the lid. Flip the turkey over and lightly spray with olive oil spray. Close the lid to continue cooking, until the internal temperature reaches at least 77ºC.
6. When cooking is complete, let the turkey rest for 10 minutes before slicing and serving.

Roasted Chicken Breast with Garlic

Prep: 5 minutes, Total Cook Time: 25 minutes, Serves: 4

INGREDIENTS:

- cooking spray
- 4 (140-g) low-sodium bone-in skinless chicken breasts
- 20 garlic cloves, unpeeled
- 27 g cornflour
- 15 ml olive oil
- 15 ml freshly squeezed lemon juice
- 1 tsp. dried basil leaves
- ⅛ tsp. freshly ground black pepper

DIRECTIONS:

1. Push in the legs on the Cook & Crisp tray, then place the tray in the bottom of the pot. Spray the tray with cooking spray.
2. Rub the chicken evenly with the olive oil and lemon juice on both sides and scatter with the cornflour, basil, and pepper.
3. Close the lid and flip the SmartSwitch to AIR FRY/HOB. Select BAKE & ROAST, set temperature to 180°C, and set time to 30 minutes (unit will need to preheat for 5 minutes, so set an external timer if desired). Press START/STOP to begin cooking.
4. When the unit is preheated and the time reaches 25 minutes, place the chicken and top with garlic cloves on the tray. Close the lid to begin cooking, until the garlic is soft and the chicken reaches an internal temperature of 74ºC on a meat thermometer.
5. Serve warm.

Simple Mexican Pork Chops

Prep Time: 5 minutes, Cook Time: 17 minutes, Serves: 2

INGREDIENTS:

- cooking spray
- ¼ tsp. dried oregano
- 1½ tsps. taco seasoning mix
- 2 (110-g) boneless pork chops
- 30 g unsalted butter, divided

DIRECTIONS:

1. Push in the legs on the Cook & Crisp tray, then place the tray in the bottom of the pot. Spray the tray with cooking spray.
2. Combine the dried oregano and taco seasoning in a small bowl and rub the mixture into the pork chops. Brush the chops with 15 g butter.
3. Close the lid and flip the SmartSwitch to AIR FRY/HOB. Select BAKE & ROAST, set temperature to 190°C, and set time to 22 minutes (unit will need to preheat for 5 minutes, so set an external timer if desired). Press START/STOP to begin cooking.
4. When the unit is preheated and the time reaches 17 minutes, place the chops on the tray. Close the lid to begin cooking.
5. After 10 minutes, open the lid and flip the chops with silicone-tipped tongs to ensure even cooking. Close the lid to continue cooking.
6. Serve with a garnish of remaining butter.

Chili Breaded Pork Chops

Prep: 5 minutes, Total Cook Time: 15 minutes, Serves: 4

INGREDIENTS:

- cooking spray
- 4 (115-g) pork chops
- 45 g bread crumbs
- 15 ml coconut oil, melted
- 1 tsp. chilli powder
- ½ tsp. garlic powder

DIRECTIONS:

1. Push in the legs on the Cook & Crisp tray, then place the tray in the bottom of the pot. Spray the tray with cooking spray.
2. Mix the chilli powder, garlic powder, and bread crumbs.
3. Coat the pork chops evenly with the coconut oil, followed by the bread crumbs mixture, taking care to cover them completely.
4. Close the lid and flip the SmartSwitch to AIR FRY/HOB. Select BAKE & ROAST, set temperature to 190°C, and set time to 20 minutes (unit will need to preheat for 5 minutes, so set an external timer if desired). Press START/STOP to begin cooking.
5. When the unit is preheated and the time reaches 15 minutes, place the chops on the tray. Close the lid to begin cooking.
6. After 10 minutes, open the lid and turn the chops over with silicone-tipped tongs to ensure even cooking. Close the lid to continue cooking.
7. Serve immediately.

Pear and Apple Crisp

Prep Time: 10 minutes, Cook Time: 20 minutes, Serves: 6

INGREDIENTS:

- cooking spray
- 225 g apples, cored and chopped
- 225 g pears, cored and chopped
- 120 g flour
- 200 g sugar
- 15 g butter
- 2 g ground cinnamon
- 0.5 g ground cloves
- 1 tsp. vanilla extract
- 25 g chopped walnuts
- Whipped cream, for serving

DIRECTIONS:

1. Push in the legs on the Cook & Crisp tray, then place the tray in the bottom of the pot. Spray Multi-Purpose Tin or 20cm cake tin with cooking spray.
2. Place the apples and pears into the tin.
3. Combine the rest of the ingredients, minus the walnuts and the whipped cream, until a coarse, crumbly texture is achieved.
4. Pour the mixture over the fruits and spread it evenly. Top with the chopped walnuts.
5. Close the lid and flip the SmartSwitch to AIR FRY/HOB. Select BAKE & ROAST, set temperature to 180°C, and set time to 25 minutes (unit will need to preheat for 5 minutes, so set an external timer if desired). Press START/STOP to begin cooking.
6. When the unit is preheated and the time reaches 20 minutes, place the tin on the tray. Close the lid to begin cooking, until the top turns golden brown.
7. Serve at room temperature with whipped cream.

Cinnamon and Pecan Pie

Prep Time: 10 minutes, Cook Time: 30 minutes, Serves: 4

INGREDIENTS:

- cooking spray
- 1 pie dough
- ½ tsps. cinnamon
- ¾ tsp. vanilla extract
- 2 eggs
- 180 ml maple syrup
- ⅛ tsp. nutmeg
- 40 g melted butter, divided
- 25 g caster sugar
- 60 g chopped pecans

DIRECTIONS:

1. Push in the legs on the Cook & Crisp tray, then place the tray in the bottom of the pot. Spray a pie pan with cooking spray.
2. In a small bowl, coat the pecans in 15 g melted butter.
3. Close the lid and flip the SmartSwitch to AIR FRY/HOB. Select BAKE & ROAST, set temperature to 190°C, and set time to 35 minutes (unit will need to preheat for 5 minutes, so set an external timer if desired). Press START/STOP to begin cooking.
4. When the unit is preheated and the time reaches 30 minutes, place the pecans on the tray. Close the lid to begin cooking.
5. With 20 minutes remaining, open the lid. Put the pie dough in the greased pie pan and add the pecans on top. In a bowl, mix the rest of the ingredients. Pour this over the pecans. Transfer the pie pan on the tray. Close the lid to continue cooking.
6. Serve immediately.

Beef Loin with Herbs

Prep Time: 5 minutes, Cook Time: 15 minutes, Serves: 4

INGREDIENTS:

- cooking spray
- 15 g butter, melted
- ¼ dried thyme
- 1 tsp. garlic salt
- ¼ tsp. dried parsley
- 450 g beef loin

DIRECTIONS:

1. Push in the legs on the Cook & Crisp tray, then place the tray in the bottom of the pot. Spray the tray with cooking spray.
2. In a bowl, combine the melted butter, thyme, garlic salt, and parsley.
3. Cut the beef loin into slices and generously apply the seasoned butter using a brush.
4. Close the lid and flip the SmartSwitch to AIR FRY/HOB. Select BAKE & ROAST, set temperature to 200°C, and set time to 20 minutes (unit will need to preheat for 5 minutes, so set an external timer if desired). Press START/STOP to begin cooking.
5. When the unit is preheated and the time reaches 15 minutes, place the beef on the tray. Close the lid to begin cooking.
6. After 8 minutes, open the lid and flip the beef with silicone-tipped tongs to ensure even cooking. Close the lid to continue cooking.
7. Take care when removing it and serve hot.

Lamb Chops with Bulb Garlic

Prep Time: 20 minutes, Cook Time: 32 minutes, Serves: 4

INGREDIENTS:

- cooking spray
- 1 tbsp. fresh oregano, chopped
- 1 tbsp. fresh thyme, chopped
- 8 (115 g each) lamb chops
- 60 ml olive oil, divided
- 1 bulb garlic
- Salt and black pepper, to taste

DIRECTIONS:

1. Push in the legs on the Cook & Crisp tray, then place the tray in the bottom of the pot. Spray the tray with cooking spray.
2. Rub the garlic bulb with about 30 ml olive oil.
3. Close the lid and flip the SmartSwitch to AIR FRY/HOB. Select BAKE & ROAST, set temperature to 200°C, and set time to 17 minutes (unit will need to preheat for 5 minutes, so set an external timer if desired). Press START/STOP to begin cooking.
4. When the unit is preheated and the time reaches 12 minutes, place the garlic bulb on the tray. Close the lid to begin cooking.
5. Mix remaining oil, herbs, salt and black pepper in a large bowl.
6. Coat the lamb chops with about 1 tbsp. of the herb mixture.
7. When cooking is complete, place half of the chops on the tray with garlic bulb and roast for 10 minutes.
8. Repeat with the remaining lamb chops and serve with herb mixture.

Classic Shortbread Fingers

Prep Time: 10 minutes, Cook Time: 12 minutes, Serves: 10

INGREDIENTS:

- cooking spray
- 200 g plain flour
- 170 g butter
- 65 g caster sugar

DIRECTIONS:

1. Push in the legs on the Cook & Crisp tray, then place the tray in the bottom of the pot. Spray the tray with cooking spray.
2. Mix sugar, flour and butter in a bowl to form a dough.
3. Cut the dough into 10 equal sized fingers and prick the fingers lightly with a fork.
4. Close the lid and flip the SmartSwitch to AIR FRY/HOB. Select BAKE & ROAST, set temperature to 180°C, and set time to 17 minutes (unit will need to preheat for 5 minutes, so set an external timer if desired). Press START/STOP to begin cooking.
5. When the unit is preheated and the time reaches 12 minutes, place the fingers on the tray. Close the lid to begin cooking.
6. Dish out and serve warm.

Buttered Striploin Steak

Prep Time: 10 minutes, Cook Time: 12 minutes, Serves: 2

INGREDIENTS:

- cooking spray
- 2 (200 g) striploin steaks
- 20 g butter, softened
- Salt and black pepper, to taste

DIRECTIONS:

1. Push in the legs on the Cook & Crisp tray, then place the tray in the bottom of the pot. Spray the tray with cooking spray.
2. Rub the steak generously with salt and black pepper and coat with butter.
3. Close the lid and flip the SmartSwitch to AIR FRY/HOB. Select BAKE & ROAST, set temperature to 200°C, and set time to 17 minutes (unit will need to preheat for 5 minutes, so set an external timer if desired). Press START/STOP to begin cooking.
4. When the unit is preheated and the time reaches 12 minutes, place the steaks on the tray. Close the lid to begin cooking.
5. After 6 minutes, open the lid and flip the steaks with silicone-tipped tongs to ensure even cooking. Close the lid to continue cooking.
6. When cooking is complete, dish out the steaks and cut into desired size slices to serve.

Tasty Mixed Nuts

Prep Time: 15 minutes, Cook Time: 14 minutes, Serves: 3

INGREDIENTS:

- cooking spray
- 75 g raw peanuts
- 60 g raw almonds
- 70 g raw cashew nuts
- 75 g sultanas
- 60 g pecans
- 15 ml olive oil
- Salt, to taste

DIRECTIONS:

1. Push in the legs on the Cook & Crisp tray, then place the tray in the bottom of the pot. Spray the tray with cooking spray.
2. Close the lid and flip the SmartSwitch to AIR FRY/HOB. Select BAKE & ROAST, set temperature to 160°C, and set time to 14 minutes (unit will need to preheat for 5 minutes, so set an external timer if desired). Press START/STOP to begin cooking.
3. When the unit is preheated and the time reaches 9 minutes, place the nuts on the tray. Close the lid to begin cooking.
4. When cooking is complete, drizzle with olive oil and salt and toss to coat well.
5. Return the nuts mixture on the tray and roast for 5 minutes.
6. Serve warm.

CHAPTER 7
DEHYDRATE

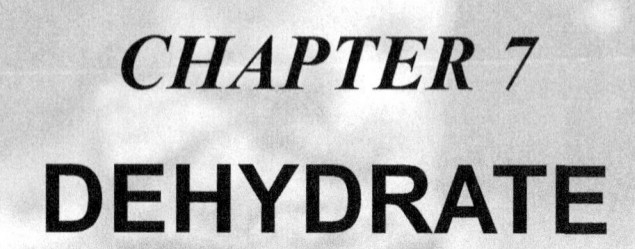

6-Hour Dehydrated Tomatoes

Prep Time: 20 minutes, Cook Time: 6 hours, Serves: 6

INGREDIENTS:

- 450 g large tomatoes, washed and cut into 3-mm slices

DIRECTIONS:

1. Spread the tomato slices on dehydrator rack.
2. Push in the legs on the Cook & Crisp tray, then place the tray in the bottom position in the pot. Put the rack with tomatoes on the tray.
3. Close the lid and flip the SmartSwitch to AIR FRY/HOB. Select DEHYDRATE, set temperature to 60°C, and set time to 6 hours. Press START/STOP to begin cooking. When done, the tomatoes should feel dry like paper, and be flexible but easily torn.
4. Remove the tomatoes from the cooker, serve immediately ou vacuum seal in vacuum bags with an oxygen pack, and then double-bagged in Mylar bag.

8-Hour Dehydrated Asparagus

Prep Time: 20 minutes, Cook Time: 8 hours, Serves: 6

INGREDIENTS:

- 450 g asparagus, washed

DIRECTIONS:

1. Remove the tough end, then boil or steam asparagus just until you can pierce the thick end with a knife; don't let it get mushy. Drain, then plunge into a large bowl of ice water until cool. Cut thick stalks into 2.5-7.5 cm pieces; thin stalks can be left whole. Spread on dehydrator rack.
2. Push in the legs on the Cook & Crisp tray, then place the tray in the bottom position in the pot. Put the rack with asparagus on the tray.
3. Close the lid and flip the SmartSwitch to AIR FRY/HOB. Select DEHYDRATE, set temperature to 60°C, and set time to 8 hours. Press START/STOP to begin cooking. When done, the asparagus should feel dry like paper and be somewhat flexible.
4. Remove the asparagus from the cooker, serve immediately ou vacuum seal in vacuum bags with an oxygen pack, and then double-bagged in Mylar bag.

Crunchy Dehydrated Brussels Sprouts

Prep Time: 20 minutes, Cook Time: 8 hours, Serves: 6

INGREDIENTS:

- 450 g Brussels sprouts, trimmed and removed any wilted leaves

DIRECTIONS:

1. Boil or steam whole Brussels sprouts until you can pierce them with a sharp knife or skewer. Drain and place the sprouts in a large bowl of ice water until cool. Cut each sprout vertically in half through the stem and spread on dehydrator rack, cut side up.
2. Push in the legs on the Cook & Crisp tray, then place the tray in the bottom position in the pot. Put the rack with Brussels sprouts on the tray.
3. Close the lid and flip the SmartSwitch to AIR FRY/HOB. Select DEHYDRATE, set temperature to 60°C, and set time to 8 hours. Press START/STOP to begin cooking. When done, the Brussels sprouts should feel dry to the touch and be crunchy.
4. Remove the Brussels sprouts from the cooker, serve immediately ou vacuum seal in vacuum bags with an oxygen pack, and then double-bagged in Mylar bag.

Crispy Dehydrated Aubergine Slices

Prep Time: 15 minutes, Cook Time: 6 hours, Serves: 6

INGREDIENTS:

- 450 g aubergines, washed and peeled

DIRECTIONS:

1. Blanch the entire aubergine in a large pot of boiling water for 15 seconds or less, then transfer it to a large bowl of ice water until cool. Cut the aubergine into 3-mmslices, then spread on dehydrator rack.
2. Push in the legs on the Cook & Crisp tray, then place the tray in the bottom position in the pot. Put the rack with aubergine on the tray.
3. Close the lid and flip the SmartSwitch to AIR FRY/HOB. Select DEHYDRATE, set temperature to 60°C, and set time to 6 hours. Press START/STOP to begin cooking. When done, the aubergine should be brittle, feel dry to the touch, and snap in half.
4. Remove the aubergine from the cooker, serve immediately ou vacuum seal in vacuum bags with an oxygen pack, and then double-bagged in Mylar bag.

Tangy Dehydrated Mango Slices

Prep Time: 20 minutes, Cook Time: 8 hours, Serves: 4

INGREDIENTS:

- spray bottle of lemon juice
- 4 large mangoes

DIRECTIONS:

1. Peel the mangoes; then, from top to bottom, cut the flesh off the large, flat seed on both sides. Cut the large pieces into wedges, or thinly slice if making mango chips, or chop. Lightly spray with lemon juice. Spread on dehydrator rack.
2. Push in the legs on the Cook & Crisp tray, then place the tray in the bottom position in the pot. Put the rack with mango on the tray.
3. Close the lid and flip the SmartSwitch to AIR FRY/HOB. Select DEHYDRATE, set temperature to 60°C, and set time to 8 hours. Press START/STOP to begin cooking. When done, the mango should feel dry like paper, be flexible, and tear easily.
4. Remove the mango from the cooker, serve immediately ou vacuum seal in vacuum bags with an oxygen pack, and then double-bagged in Mylar bag.

Crispy Dehydrated Banana Chips

Prep Time: 10 minutes, Cook Time: 7 hours, Serves: 4

INGREDIENTS:

- spray bottle of lemon juice
- 4 medium bananas, peeled and cut across into 3-mm-thick slices

DIRECTIONS:

1. Lightly spray the banana slices with lemon juice, spread on dehydrator rack.
2. Push in the legs on the Cook & Crisp tray, then place the tray in the bottom position in the pot. Put the rack with banana chips on the tray.
3. Close the lid and flip the SmartSwitch to AIR FRY/HOB. Select DEHYDRATE, set temperature to 60°C, and set time to 7 hours. Press START/STOP to begin cooking. When done, the banana chips should be brittle, feel dry to the touch, and snap in half easily.
4. Remove the banana chips from the cooker, serve immediately ou vacuum seal in vacuum bags with an oxygen pack, and then double-bagged in Mylar bag.

Crunchy Dehydrated Carrot Slices

Prep Time: 15 minutes, Cook Time: 8 hours, Serves: 6

INGREDIENTS:

- spray bottle of lemon juice
- 450 g carrots, trimmed and peeled

DIRECTIONS:

1. Blanch carrots in a large pot of boiling water for 5 minutes, and no longer (they are ready when they turn bright orange). Drain and place in a large bowl of ice water to cool. Cut the carrots into 1-cm slices. Lightly spray with lemon juice, spread on dehydrator rack.
2. Push in the legs on the Cook & Crisp tray, then place the tray in the bottom position in the pot. Put the rack with carrots on the tray.
3. Close the lid and flip the SmartSwitch to AIR FRY/HOB. Select DEHYDRATE, set temperature to 60°C, and set time to 8 hours. Press START/STOP to begin cooking. When done, the carrots should feel hard and dry to the touch, but still be somewhat flexible.
4. Remove the carrots from the cooker, serve immediately ou vacuum seal in vacuum bags with an oxygen pack, and then double-bagged in Mylar bag.

Dehydrated Dragon Fruit

Prep Time: 20 minutes, Cook Time: 6 hours, Serves: 6

INGREDIENTS:

- 3 large Dragon Fruits, washed thoroughly, cut into 0.5 cm slices and
  left the skin on the fruit (can hold the slices together)

DIRECTIONS:

1. Spread the fruit slices on dehydrator rack.
2. Push in the legs on the Cook & Crisp tray, then place the tray in the bottom position in the pot. Put the rack with fruit slices on the tray.
3. Close the lid and flip the SmartSwitch to AIR FRY/HOB. Select DEHYDRATE, set temperature to 60°C, and set time to 6 hours. Press START/STOP to begin cooking. When done, the fruit slices should feel dry like paper, be flexible, and tear easily.
4. Remove the fruit slices from the cooker, serve immediately ou vacuum seal in vacuum bags with an oxygen pack, and then double-bagged in Mylar bag.

Crunchy Dehydrated Olives

Prep Time: 10 minutes, Cook Time: 8 hours, Serves: 6

INGREDIENTS:

- 450 g green olives, drained and pitted

DIRECTIONS:

1. Spread the olives on dehydrator rack.
2. Push in the legs on the Cook & Crisp tray, then place the tray in the bottom position in the pot. Put the rack with olives on the tray.
3. Close the lid and flip the SmartSwitch to AIR FRY/HOB. Select DEHYDRATE, set temperature to 60°C, and set time to 8 hours. Press START/STOP to begin cooking. When done, the olives should feel dry like paper and be somewhat flexible but will snap if bent in half.
4. Remove the olives from the cooker, serve immediately ou vacuum seal in vacuum bags with an oxygen pack, and then double-bagged in Mylar bag.

Dehydrated Kiwi Fruit

Prep Time: 20 minutes, Cook Time: 8 hours, Serves: 6

INGREDIENTS:

- spray bottle of lemon juice
- 6 medium kiwi fruits, peeled and sliced as thinly as you can

DIRECTIONS:

1. Lightly spray the kiwi slices with lemon juice, spread on dehydrator rack.
2. Push in the legs on the Cook & Crisp tray, then place the tray in the bottom position in the pot. Put the rack with kiwi slices on the tray.
3. Close the lid and flip the SmartSwitch to AIR FRY/HOB. Select DEHYDRATE, set temperature to 60°C, and set time to 8 hours. Press START/STOP to begin cooking. When done, the kiwi should feel dry like paper, be flexible, and tear easily.
4. Remove the kiwi from the cooker, place in ziptop plastic freezer bags and seal, trying to remove as much air as possible. Double-bag inside a Mylar bag, or store inside a canning jar with a lid and oxygen pack.

Dehydrated Strawberry Slices

Prep Time: 20 minutes, Cook Time: 7 hours, Serves: 6

INGREDIENTS:

- spray bottle of lemon juice
- 450 g strawberries, washed and hulled, then thin sliced

DIRECTIONS:

1. Lightly spray the strawberries with lemon juice. Spread on dehydrator rack.
2. Push in the legs on the Cook & Crisp tray, then place the tray in the bottom position in the pot. Put the rack with strawberries on the tray.
3. Close the lid and flip the SmartSwitch to AIR FRY/HOB. Select DEHYDRATE, set temperature to 60°C, and set time to 7 hours. Press START/STOP to begin cooking. When done, the strawberries should feel dry like paper and be somewhat flexible.
4. Remove the strawberries from the cooker, serve immediately ou vacuum seal in vacuum bags with an oxygen pack, and then double-bagged in Mylar bag.

Sweet and Spicy Pepper Beef Jerky

Prep Time: 20 minutes, Cook Time: 6 hours 15 minutes, Makes: 225 g jerky

INGREDIENTS:

- 680 g beef eye of round
- 120 ml pineapple juice
- 50 g firmly packed brown sugar
- 60 ml soy sauce
- 1 tbsp. crushed dehydrated jalapeños
- 5 ml hot sauce

DIRECTIONS:

1. Trim the meat of any visible fat, then partially freeze. Cut into 0.5-cm-thick slices or strips across the grain using a very sharp knife or meat slicer. Try to cut the meat as uniformly as possible for even drying. Place the strips in a large ziptop plastic freezer bag.
2. While the meat freezes, combine the remaining ingredients in a small saucepan. Place over medium heat and stir until the sugar dissolves. Let cool, then carefully pour over the strips in the bag. Squish everything around to coat, then seal the bag and refrigerate until the meat is no longer red, about 24 hours, turning and squishing the bag about halfway through to ensure even coverage with the marinade.
3. Drain off the marinade and place the strips in a single layer on dehydrator rack.
4. Push in the legs on the Cook & Crisp tray, then place the tray in the bottom position in the pot. Put the rack with jerk on the tray.
5. Close the lid and flip the SmartSwitch to AIR FRY/HOB. Select DEHYDRATE, set temperature to 70°C, and set time to 6 hours. Press START/STOP to begin cooking. When done, the jerky should bend but not snap, and show no signs of redness.
6. Remove the jerky from the cooker, arrange on baking sheets in a single layer, and place in a preheated 135°C oven for 15 minutes. Allow the jerky to cool completely before placing in an airtight container.

Smoky Salmon Jerky

Prep Time: 30 minutes, Cook Time: 7 hours 15 minutes, Makes: 225 g jerky

INGREDIENTS:

- 680 g salmon fillets, skin and pin bones removed
- 120 ml soy sauce
- 1 tbsp. molasses
- 15 ml lemon juice
- 15 ml Worcestershire sauce
- 2 tsps. black pepper
- 1 tsp. liquid smoke

DIRECTIONS:

1. Partially freeze the fillets, then cut across into ½ to 1 cm-thick slices or strips using a very sharp knife or meat slicer. Try to cut the salmon as uniformly as possible for even drying. Place the strips in a large zip-top plastic freezer bag.
2. Whisk the remaining ingredients together in a small bowl and carefully pour over the strips in the bag. Squish everything around to coat, then seal the bag and refrigerate for 3 to 6 hours (no longer, or you run the risk of the salmon becoming mushy), turning and squishing the bag about halfway through to ensure even coverage with the marinade.
3. Drain off the marinade and place the strips in a single layer on dehydrator rack.
4. Push in the legs on the Cook & Crisp tray, then place the tray in the bottom position in the pot. Put the rack with jerk on the tray.
5. Close the lid and flip the SmartSwitch to AIR FRY/HOB. Select DEHYDRATE, set temperature to 70°C, and set time to 7 hours. Press START/STOP to begin cooking. When done, the jerky should bend but not snap.
6. Remove the jerky from the cooker, arrange on baking sheets in a single layer, and place in a preheated 135°C oven for 15 minutes. Allow the jerky to cool completely before placing in an airtight container.

Sweet and Sour Chicken Jerky

Prep Time: 20 minutes, Cook Time: 6 hours 15 minutes, Makes: 225 g jerky

INGREDIENTS:

- 680 g boneless, skinless chicken breasts, trimmed of all visible fat
- 55 g firmly packed brown sugar
- 60 ml distilled white vinegar
- 60 ml pineapple juice
- 1 tbsp. powdered dehydrated onions
- 4 fresh garlic cloves, peeled and crushed
- 1 tbsp. soy sauce

DIRECTIONS:

1. Partially freeze the chicken breasts, then cut into 0.5-cm-thick slices or strips using a very sharp knife or meat slicer. Try to cut them as uniformly as possible for even drying. Place the strips in a large ziptop plastic freezer bag.
2. Whisk the remaining ingredients together in a small bowl and carefully pour over the strips in the bag. Squish everything around to coat, then seal the bag and refrigerate for at least 12 hours, turning and squishing the bag about halfway through to ensure even coverage with the marinade.
3. Drain off the marinade and place the strips in a single layer on dehydrator rack.
4. Push in the legs on the Cook & Crisp tray, then place the tray in the bottom position in the pot. Put the rack with jerk on the tray.
5. Close the lid and flip the SmartSwitch to AIR FRY/HOB. Select DEHYDRATE, set temperature to 70°C, and set time to 6 hours. Press START/STOP to begin cooking. When done, the jerky should bend but not snap.
6. Remove the jerky from the cooker, arrange on baking sheets in a single layer, and place in a preheated 135°C oven for 15 minutes. Allow the jerky to cool completely before placing in an airtight container.

Spicy Sriracha Turkey Jerky

Prep Time: 15 minutes, Cook Time: 7 hours 15 minutes, Makes: 225 g jerky

INGREDIENTS:

- 680 g boneless, skinless turkey breast, trimmed of all visible fat
- 160 ml soy sauce
- 45 ml honey
- 60 ml sriracha
- 2 tsps. red pepper flakes

DIRECTIONS:

1. Partially freeze the turkey breast, then cut into 0.5-cm-thick slices or strips using a very sharp knife or meat slicer. Try to cut it as uniformly as possible for even drying. Place the strips in a large ziptop plastic freezer bag.
2. Whisk the remaining ingredients together in a small bowl and carefully pour over the strips in the bag. Squish everything around to coat, then seal the bag and refrigerate for 12 hours, turning and squishing the bag about halfway through to ensure even coverage with the marinade.
3. Drain off the marinade and place the strips in a single layer on dehydrator rack. Push in the legs on the Cook & Crisp tray, then place the tray in the bottom position in the pot. Put the rack with jerk on the tray.
4. Close the lid and flip the SmartSwitch to AIR FRY/HOB. Select DEHYDRATE, set temperature to 70°C, and set time to 7 hours. Press START/STOP to begin cooking. When done, the jerky should bend but not snap.
5. Remove the jerky from the cooker, arrange on baking sheets in a single layer, and place in a preheated 135°C oven for 15 minutes. Allow the jerky to cool completely before placing in an airtight container.

CHAPTER 8
SEARSAUTÉ

Cranberry Beef Stir-Fry with Veggies

Prep Time: 25 minutes, Cook Time: 19 minutes, Serves: 6

INGREDIENTS:

- 1 (400-g) tin jellied cranberry sauce
- 45 ml olive oil
- 30 ml lemon juice
- 1 tbsp. minced garlic
- 75 g broccoli florets
- 900 g cubed beef stew meat
- 75 g sliced carrot
- 1 tsp. ground ginger
- 75 g sugar snap peas
- 75 g sliced onion

DIRECTIONS:

1. Before getting started, be sure to remove the Cook & Crisp tray from the pot.
2. In a small mixing bowl, combine the lemon juice with cranberry sauce.
3. Flip the SmartSwitch to AIR FRY/HOB. Select SEAR/SAUTÉ and set to 4. Press START/STOP to begin cooking.
4. Add a splash of oil in the pot. Place the broccoli, carrot, snap peas, and onion. Sauté them for 6 minutes. Set the mixture aside.
5. Add oil in the pot. Sauté the garlic for 1 minutes. Add the beef and cook for 6 minutes.
6. Place the cooked veggies with ginger and cranberry sauce mixture. Cook them for 6 minutes. Serve warm.

New England Fried Chips and Fried Fish

Prep Time: 10 minutes, Cook Time: 10 minutes, Serves: 4

INGREDIENTS:

- 120 g plain flour
- 1 tsp. baking powder
- 1 L vegetable oil
- Salt and freshly ground black pepper, to taste
- 680 g cod fillets
- 1 egg, beaten lightly
- 240 ml milk
- 4 large potatoes, peeled and cut into strips lengthwise

DIRECTIONS:

1. Before getting started, be sure to remove the Cook & Crisp tray from the pot.
2. In a large bowl, add flour, baking powder, salt, black pepper, egg and milk.
3. Mix until well combined.
4. Keep everything aside for at least 20 minutes.
5. In a large bowl of chilled water, dip the potatoes for 2 to 3 minutes.
6. Drain the mix well and pat dry with paper towel.
7. Flip the SmartSwitch to AIR FRY/HOB. Select SEAR/SAUTÉ and set to 3. Press START/STOP to begin cooking.
8. Heat the oil in the pot. Add the potatoes and sauté for about 3 to 4 minutes or until crisp and tender.
9. Transfer the potatoes onto a paper towel lined plate.
10. Coat the cod fillets in the flour mixture evenly.
11. Sauté everything for about 3 to 4 minutes or until golden brown.
12. Transfer the cod fillets onto another paper towel lined plate.
13. Now, return the potato strips to the pot and cook for about 1 to 2 minutes more or until crispy.

Salt and Pepper Prawn

Prep Time: 5 minutes, Cook Time: 5 minutes, Serves: 4 to 6

INGREDIENTS:

- 30 g cornflour
- 1 tsp. freshly ground black pepper
- 1 tsp. sea salt
- 450 g large prawns, deveined, tail on
- 30 ml peanut oil
- ½ red chilli or 1 Thai bird's eye chile, thinly sliced (optional)
- 1 sprig fresh coriander, roughly chopped

DIRECTIONS:

1. Before getting started, be sure to remove the Cook & Crisp tray from the pot.
2. In a medium bowl, combine the cornflour, pepper, and sea salt. Mix well and set it aside.
3. Just before frying the prawns, add the prawns to the cornflour mixture and toss to coat.
4. Flip the SmartSwitch to AIR FRY/HOB. Select SEAR/SAUTÉ and set to 4. Press START/STOP to begin cooking.
5. Heat the peanut oil in the pot.
6. Shake any excess cornflour off the prawns and place them in the pot in a single layer.
7. Allow the prawn to sear on one side for about 30 seconds before flipping.
8. Add the sliced red chilli or Thai bird's eye chile to the pot (if using) and gently stir-fry to combine.
9. Transfer to a serving dish and garnish with the coriander.

Sichuan Pork and Bell Pepper with Peanuts

Prep Time: 8 minutes, Cook Time: 5 minutes, Serves: 4

INGREDIENTS:

- 450 g pork, minced
- 1 medium onion, cut into 2.5 cm pieces
- 1 medium red bell pepper, cut into 2.5 cm pieces
- 65 g peanuts
- 2 garlic cloves, crushed and chopped
- 30 ml cooking oil
- 30 ml rice wine
- 30 ml rice vinegar
- 1 tbsp. ginger, crushed and chopped
- 1 tbsp. Chinese five-spice powder
- 1 tbsp. cornflour
- 1 tsp. red pepper flakes
- 5 ml hot sesame oil

DIRECTIONS:

1. Before getting started, be sure to remove the Cook & Crisp tray from the pot.
2. Flip the SmartSwitch to AIR FRY/HOB. Select SEAR/SAUTÉ and set to HI-5. Press START/STOP to begin cooking.
3. Heat the cooking oil in the pot until it shimmers.
4. Put the garlic, ginger, pork and onion and sear for about 2 minutes.
5. Place the red pepper flakes, five-spice powder, sesame oil and bell pepper and sauté for about 1 minute.
6. Toss the rice wine, rice vinegar and cornflour and stir until a glaze is formed.
7. Add the peanuts and give a stir. Serve warm.

Corned Beef

Prep Time: 15 minutes, Cook Time: 15 minutes, Serves: 4

INGREDIENTS:

- 1 (340-g) tin corned beef
- ¼ onion, chopped
- ¼ green bell pepper, chopped
- 60 ml water
- 10 ml tomato paste
- 5 ml vegetable oil
- ¼ tsp. dried thyme
- ¼ tsp. crushed red pepper flakes
- Salt and pepper to taste

DIRECTIONS:

1. Before getting started, be sure to remove the Cook & Crisp tray from the pot.
2. Flip the SmartSwitch to AIR FRY/HOB. Select SEAR/SAUTÉ and set to 3. Press START/STOP to begin cooking.
3. In the pot, heat the oil. Add the green pepper, onion, red pepper flakes and dried thyme and sauté for 7 minutes.
4. Set to LO-1 and toss in the tomato paste, salt and pepper. Simmer for 3 minutes.
5. Stir in the corned beef and water and simmer until all the liquid is absorbed. Serve warm.

Ginger Lentil Stew

Prep Time: 10 minutes, Cook Time: 35 minutes, Serves: 6

INGREDIENTS:

- 360 g orange lentils, rinsed
- 1 tsp. crushed cumin seed
- ½ tsp. salt
- 1 tsp. crushed cardamom seed
- 60 ml vegetable oil
- ¼ tsp. ground cinnamon
- 1 large sweet onion, chopped
- ½ tsp. cayenne pepper
- 2.5 cm piece fresh ginger, grated
- 240 g fresh tomato, diced peeled
- 3 garlic cloves, crushed
- 1 tsp. coriander powder
- 1 tsp. turmeric

DIRECTIONS:

1. Before getting started, be sure to remove the Cook & Crisp tray from the pot.
2. Flip the SmartSwitch to AIR FRY/HOB. Select SEAR/SAUTÉ and set to 3. Press START/STOP to begin cooking.
3. Stir the lentils with salt in the pot. Cover them with boiling water.
4. Let the lentils cook for 22 minutes.
5. Once the time is up, drain the lentils. Place it in a mixing bowl and press it with a potato masher to mash it slightly.
6. Heat the oil in the pot. Sauté the onion with garlic for 5 minutes.
7. Stir in the rest of the ingredients. Cook them for 6 minutes. Add the lentils and heat them through.
8. Serve your lentils stew warm.

Sesame Asparagus

Prep Time: 5 minutes, Cook Time: 6 minutes, Serves: 4

INGREDIENTS:

- 2 tbsps. light soy sauce
- 1 tsp. caster sugar
- 15 ml vegetable oil
- 2 large garlic cloves, coarsely chopped
- 900 g asparagus, trimmed and cut diagonally into 5 cm-long pieces
- coarse salt
- 30 ml sesame oil
- 1 tbsp. toasted sesame seeds

DIRECTIONS:

1. Before getting started, be sure to remove the Cook & Crisp tray from the pot.
2. In a small bowl, stir the light soy and caster sugar together until the sugar dissolves. Set aside.
3. Flip the SmartSwitch to AIR FRY/HOB. Select SEAR/SAUTÉ and set to 4. Press START/STOP to begin cooking.
4. Pour in the vegetable oil in the pot. Add the garlic and sauté until fragrant, about 10 seconds.
5. Add the asparagus and sauté until crisp-tender, about 4 minutes, seasoning with a small pinch of salt while sautéing. Add the soy sauce mixture and toss to coat the asparagus, cooking for about 1 minute more.
6. Drizzle the sesame oil over the asparagus and transfer to a serving bowl. Garnish with the sesame seeds and serve hot.

Little Bay Yellow Curry

Prep Time: 15 minutes, Cook Time: 40 minutes, Serves: 4

INGREDIENTS:

- 30 ml vegetable oil
- 2½ tbsps. yellow curry powder
- 1 white onion, chopped
- 1 tsp. garlic salt
- 2 cloves garlic, crushed
- 1 (400 g) tin unsweetened coconut milk
- 450 g skinless, boneless chicken breast halves, chopped
- 80 ml chicken stock
- Salt and pepper to taste
- 1 small head cauliflower, chopped

DIRECTIONS:

1. Before getting started, be sure to remove the Cook & Crisp tray from the pot.
2. Flip the SmartSwitch to AIR FRY/HOB. Select SEAR/SAUTÉ and set to 3. Press START/STOP to begin cooking.
3. Heat the oil in the pot, sauté the onion and garlic until tender.
4. Stir in the chicken and sear for about 10 minutes.
5. Stir in the cauliflower, curry powder, garlic salt, coconut milk, chicken stock, salt and pepper.
6. Set to LO-1 and simmer for about 30 minutes, stirring occasionally.
7. Serve hot.

Thai Basil Pork Bowls

Prep Time: 7 minutes, Cook Time: 5 minutes, Serves: 4

INGREDIENTS:

- 450 g pork, minced
- 1 medium red bell pepper, cut into 1 cm pieces
- 1 handful fresh Thai basil leaves
- 2 garlic cloves, crushed and chopped
- 30 ml cooking oil
- 1 tbsp. ginger, crushed and chopped
- 15 ml fish sauce
- 25 g brown sugar
- 15 ml soy sauce

DIRECTIONS:

1. Before getting started, be sure to remove the Cook & Crisp tray from the pot.
2. Flip the SmartSwitch to AIR FRY/HOB. Select SEAR/SAUTÉ and set to HI-5. Press START/STOP to begin cooking.
3. Heat the cooking oil in the pot until it shimmers.
4. Add the garlic, ginger and pork and sear for about 2 minutes.
5. Pour the bell pepper, brown sugar, fish sauce and soy sauce and sauté for about 1 minute.
6. Sprinkle the basil and sauté until just wilted.
7. Serve warm.

Hoisin Tofu

Prep Time: 5 minutes, Cook Time: 2 minutes, Serves: 2 to 4

INGREDIENTS:

For the Sauce:
- 30 ml hoisin sauce
- 15 ml honey
- 10 ml sesame oil
- 5 ml soy sauce

For the Stir-Fry:
- 30 ml peanut oil
- 1 block firm tofu, cut into 2-4 cm cubes (about 400 g)
- 5 g toasted sesame seeds
- 1 scallion, chopped

DIRECTIONS:

1. Before getting started, be sure to remove the Cook & Crisp tray from the pot.
2. In a small bowl, make the sauce by combining the hoisin sauce, honey, sesame oil, and soy sauce. Set it aside.
3. Flip the SmartSwitch to AIR FRY/HOB. Select SEAR/SAUTÉ and set to 4 Press START/STOP to begin cooking.
4. Heat the peanut oil in the pot.
5. Carefully drop the tofu cubes into the pot, and allow the bottom side to sear for about 20 seconds before gently flipping them over.
6. When the tofu is cooked on all sides, top with the sauce, gently stirring to coat the tofu cubes.
7. Transfer the tofu to a serving plate. Garnish with the sesame seeds and chopped scallion.

Chicken Pomegranate Stew

Prep Time: 15 minutes, Cook Time: 2 hours, Serves: 6

INGREDIENTS:

- 30 ml olive oil
- ½ tsp. cardamom (optional)
- 1 (225-g) chicken legs, cut up
- 25 g caster sugar (optional)
- 1 white onion, thinly sliced
- 225 g walnuts, toasted and finely ground in a food processor
- 1 tsp. salt
- 900 ml pomegranate juice

DIRECTIONS:

1. Before getting started, be sure to remove the Cook & Crisp tray from the pot.
2. Flip the SmartSwitch to AIR FRY/HOB. Select SEAR/SAUTÉ and set to 3. Press START/STOP to begin cooking.
3. Heat the olive oil in the pot. Sauté onions, and chicken for 20 minutes.
4. Add cardamom, walnut purée, pomegranate juice, and salt.
5. Heat until boiling. Set to LO-1 and cover the pot. Let everything simmer for 1½ hours.
6. Add some sugar. Simmer for 30 more minutes.
7. Serve and enjoy.

Garlic Kimchi Chicken and Cabbage

Prep Time: 8 minutes, Cook Time: 5 minutes, Serves: 4

INGREDIENTS:

- 450 g chicken, minced
- 225 g chopped kimchi
- 2 heads baby bok choy, leaves separated
- 2 garlic cloves, crushed and chopped
- 30 ml cooking oil
- 2 tbsps. sesame seeds
- 1 tbsp. ginger, crushed and chopped
- 1 tbsp. fish sauce
- 1 tbsp. gochujang
- 15 ml toasted sesame oil

DIRECTIONS:

1. Before getting started, be sure to remove the Cook & Crisp tray from the pot.
2. Flip the SmartSwitch to AIR FRY/HOB. Select SEAR/SAUTÉ and set to HI-5. Press START/STOP to begin cooking.
3. Heat the cooking oil in the pot until it shimmers.
4. Add the garlic, ginger, and chicken and sear for about 2 minutes.
5. Put the kimchi, bok choy, gochujang and fish sauce and sauté for about 1 minute.
6. Pour in the sesame oil and sesame seeds and toss.
7. Serve hot.

Brussels Sprouts with Pistachios

Prep Time: 15 minutes, Cook Time: 15 minutes, Serves: 6

INGREDIENTS:

- 1.8 kg Brussels sprouts
- Salt and pepper to taste
- 115 g unsalted butter
- 65 g coarsely chopped pistachios
- 4 small red onions, cut into strips
- 60 ml red wine vinegar
- 20 g caster sugar

DIRECTIONS:

1. Before getting started, be sure to remove the Cook & Crisp tray from the pot.
2. Arrange a steamer basket in a pan of the boiling water.
3. Place the Brussels sprouts in the steamer basket and cook, covered for about 8 to 10 minutes.
4. Flip the SmartSwitch to AIR FRY/HOB. Select SEAR/SAUTÉ and set to 3. Press START/STOP to begin cooking.
5. Melt the butter in the pot and sauté the onions and 45 ml of the vinegar until the onions are browned.
6. Add the Brussels sprouts, sugar and the remaining vinegar and sauté until the Brussels sprouts are lightly caramelised.
7. Season with the salt and pepper and press START/STOP to turn off the cooker.
8. Serve with a garnishing of the pistachios.

Lime Lamb and Scallions

Prep Time: 11 minutes, Cook Time: 5 minutes, Serves: 4

INGREDIENTS:

- 450 g lamb tenderloin, cut into 2.5 cm pieces, across the grain
- 1 medium onion, diced
- 2 or 3 Thai bird's eye chiles
- Juice of 1 lime
- 4 scallions, cut into 2.5 cm pieces
- 2 garlic cloves, crushed and chopped
- 30 ml cooking oil
- 15 ml hot sesame oil
- 1 tbsp. ginger, crushed and chopped
- 12 g brown sugar
- 15 ml fish sauce
- 15 ml soy sauce
- 8 g cornflour

DIRECTIONS:

1. Before getting started, be sure to remove the Cook & Crisp tray from the pot.
2. Whisk together the lime juice, brown sugar, sesame oil and cornflour in a small bowl. Keep aside.
3. Combine the soy sauce and fish sauce in a large bowl. Add the lamb and massage for about 1 minute.
4. Flip the SmartSwitch to AIR FRY/HOB. Select SEAR/SAUTÉ and set to HI-5. Press START/STOP to begin cooking.
5. Heat the cooking oi in the pot until it shimmers.
6. Add the garlic, ginger and lamb and sear for about 1 minute.
7. Place the bird's eye chiles and onion and sauté for about 1 minute.
8. Pour in the lime juice mixture and stir until a glaze is formed.
9. Sprinkle with the scallions and serve warm.

Sichuan Cumin-Spiced Lamb

Prep Time: 20 minutes, Cook Time: 15 minutes, Serves: 4

INGREDIENTS:

- 340 g boneless leg of lamb, cut into 2.5 cm pieces
- 6 to 8 whole dried Chinese chili peppers (optional)
- ½ yellow onion, sliced lengthwise into strips
- 4 peeled fresh ginger slices, each about the size of a quarter
- 4 garlic cloves, thinly sliced
- ½ bunch fresh coriander, coarsely chopped
- 45 ml vegetable oil, divided
- 15 g cornflour
- 15 g ground cumin
- 15 ml light soy sauce
- 15 ml Shaoxing rice wine
- 1 tsp. Sichuan peppercorns, crushed
- ½ tsp. sugar
- coarse salt

DIRECTIONS:

1. Combine the lamb, rice wine, light soy, and a small pinch of salt in a mixing bowl. Toss to coat well and marinate for 15 minutes, or overnight in the refrigerator.
2. Stir together the cumin, Sichuan peppercorns and sugar in another bowl. Keep aside.
3. Before getting started, be sure to remove the Cook & Crisp tray from the pot.
4. Flip the SmartSwitch to AIR FRY/HOB. Select SEAR/SAUTÉ and set to HI-5. Press START/STOP to begin cooking.
5. Heat the pot until a drop of water sizzles and evaporates on contact.
6. Add 30 ml oil and swirl to coat the base of the pot well. Season the oil with the ginger and a pinch of salt. Let the ginger sizzle in the oil for 30 seconds, swirling slowly.
7. Toss the lamb pieces with the cornflour and add them to the hot pot. Sear the lamb for about 2 to 3 minutes per side, and then sauté for 1 or 2 minutes more, gently tossing and flipping around the pot. Transfer the lamb to a clean bowl and keep aside.
8. Pour in the remaining 1 tbsp. of oil and swirl to coat the pot well. Toss in the onion and chili peppers (if using) and sauté for about 3 to 4 minutes, or until the onion begins to turn shiny but not limp. Season lightly with a small pinch of salt. Stir in the garlic and spice mixture and continue to sauté for 1 minute.
9. Take the lamb back to the pot and toss to combine for about 1 to 2 minutes more. Transfer the lamb to a platter. Remove and discard the ginger and garnish with the coriander. Serve warm.

CHAPTER 9
SLOW COOK

Peach Brown Betty with Cranberries

Prep Time: 20 minutes, Cook Time: 6 hours, Serves: 10

INGREDIENTS:

- 80 ml melted coconut oil
- 8 ripe peaches, peeled and cut into chunks
- 360 g cubed whole-wheat bread
- 180 g whole-wheat bread crumbs
- 140 g dried cranberries
- 70 g coconut sugar
- 45 ml honey
- 30 ml freshly squeezed lemon juice
- ¼ tsp. ground cardamom

DIRECTIONS:

1. Before getting started, be sure to remove the Cook & Crisp tray.
2. Mix the peaches, dried cranberries, lemon juice, and honey in the bottom of the pot.
3. In a large bowl, mix the bread crumbs, bread cubes, coconut sugar, and cardamom. Pour the melted coconut oil over all and toss to coat well.
4. Place the bread mixture on the fruit in the pot.
5. Close the lid and flip the SmartSwitch to AIR FRY/HOB. Select SLOW COOK, set temperature to LOW, and set time to 6 hours. Press START/STOP to begin cooking, until the fruit is bubbling and the topping is browned.
6. Serve warm.

Mustard Beef Brisket

Prep Time: 15 minutes, Cook Time: 10 hours, Serves: 12

INGREDIENTS:

- 1 (1.4-kg) grass-fed beef brisket, trimmed
- 2 (225-g) BPA-free tins no-salt-added tomato sauce
- 80 ml natural mustard
- 3 onions, chopped
- 8 garlic cloves, minced
- 45 ml honey
- 2 tsps. paprika
- 1 tsp. dried marjoram leaves
- 1 tsp. dried oregano leaves
- ½ tsp. cayenne pepper

DIRECTIONS:

1. Before getting started, be sure to remove the Cook & Crisp tray.
2. Add the onions and garlic to the bottom of the pot.
3. In a small bowl, mix the oregano, marjoram, paprika, and cayenne. Gently rub this mixture into the beef brisket.
4. Mix the tomato sauce, mustard, and honey until well combined in another small bowl.
5. Place the beef on the onions and garlic in the pot. Add the tomato mixture over all.
6. Close the lid and flip the SmartSwitch to AIR FRY/HOB. Select SLOW COOK, set temperature to LOW, and set time to 10 hours. Press START/STOP to begin cooking, until the beef is very soft.
7. Slice or shred the beef and serve it on buns.

Moroccan Beef Tagine and Carrot

Prep Time: 15 minutes, Cook Time: 8 hours, Serves: 8 to 10

INGREDIENTS:

- 1 (1.4-kg) grass-fed beef sirloin roast, cut into 5 cm pieces
- 3 carrots, cut into chunks
- 160 g chopped dates
- 2 red chillies, minced
- 2 onions, chopped
- 250 ml beef stock
- 6 garlic cloves, minced
- 30 ml honey
- 10 g ground cumin
- 5 g ground turmeric

DIRECTIONS:

1. Before getting started, be sure to remove the Cook & Crisp tray.
2. Add the onions, garlic, red chillies, carrots, and dates to the bottom of the pot.
3. In a small bowl, mix the beef stock, honey, cumin, and turmeric until combined well. Pour the mixture into the pot.
4. Close the lid and flip the SmartSwitch to AIR FRY/HOB. Select SLOW COOK, set temperature to LOW, and set time to 8 hours. Press START/STOP to begin cooking, until the beef is soft.
5. Enjoy!

Chicken Breast with Artichokes and Bell Pepper

Prep Time: 8 minutes, Cook Time: 6 hours, Serves: 4 to 6

INGREDIENTS:

- 8 (170-g) boneless, skinless chicken breasts
- 2 (400-g) BPA-free tins no-salt-added artichoke hearts, drained
- 2 red bell peppers, stemmed, seeded, and chopped
- 2 leeks, chopped
- 250 ml chicken stock
- 8 g chopped flat-leaf parsley
- 3 garlic cloves, minced
- 30 ml lemon juice
- 1 tsp. dried basil leaves

DIRECTIONS:

1. Before getting started, be sure to remove the Cook & Crisp tray.
2. Layer the leeks, garlic, artichoke hearts, bell peppers, chicken, stock, lemon juice, and basil in the bottom of the pot.
3. Close the lid and flip the SmartSwitch to AIR FRY/HOB. Select SLOW COOK, set temperature to LOW, and set time to 6 hours. Press START/STOP to begin cooking, until the chicken registers 75ºC on a food thermometer.
4. Garnish with the parsley and serve warm.

Healthy Spinach Porridge

Prep Time: 12 minutes, Cook Time: 8 hours, Serves: 6 to 8

INGREDIENTS:

- 300 g coarse oatmeal
- 150 g chopped baby spinach leaves
- 50 g grated Parmesan cheese
- 1.2 L vegetable broth
- 250 ml water
- 2 shallots, peeled and minced
- 2 tbsps. chopped fresh basil
- 1 tsp. dried basil leaves
- ½ tsp. dried thyme leaves
- ¼ tsp. Salt
- ¼ tsp. freshly ground black pepper

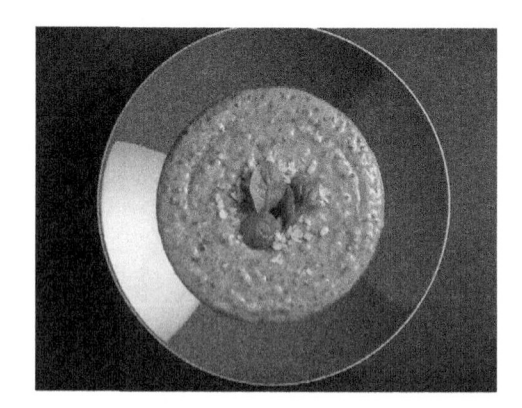

DIRECTIONS:

1. Before getting started, be sure to remove the Cook & Crisp tray.
2. Mix the coarse oatmeal, shallots, vegetable broth, water, basil, thyme, salt, and pepper in the bottom of the pot.
3. Close the lid and flip the SmartSwitch to AIR FRY/HOB. Select SLOW COOK, set temperature to LOW, and set time to 8 hours. Press START/STOP to begin cooking, until the oatmeal is soft.
4. Stir in the spinach, Parmesan cheese, and basil, and allow to stand, covered, for another 5 minutes. Stir and serve warm.

Vegan Quinoa Egg Casserole

Prep Time: 13 minutes, Cook Time: 7 hours, Serves: 6 to 8

INGREDIENTS:

- 11 eggs
- 225 g chopped kale
- 710 ml semi-skimmed milk
- 225 g quinoa, rinsed and drained
- 375 ml vegetable broth
- 170 g shredded Havarti cheese
- 1 red bell pepper, stemmed, seeded, and chopped
- 1 leek, chopped
- 3 garlic cloves, minced
- vegetable oil for greasing

DIRECTIONS:

1. Before getting started, be sure to remove the Cook & Crisp tray.
2. Grease the bottom of the pot lightly with vegetable oil and keep aside.
3. Mix the milk, vegetable broth, and eggs in a large bowl, and beat well with a wire whisk.
4. Stir in the kale, quinoa, leek, bell pepper, garlic, and cheese. Add this mixture into the pot.
5. Close the lid and flip the SmartSwitch to AIR FRY/HOB. Select SLOW COOK, set temperature to LOW, and set time to 7 hours. Press START/STOP to begin cooking, until a food thermometer registers 74ºC and the mixture is set.
6. Serve warm.

Thai Chicken with Greens

Prep Time: 10 minutes, Cook Time: 8 hours, Serves: 6 to 8

INGREDIENTS:

- 2 (450-g) packages prepared collard greens
- 10 (110-g) boneless, skinless chicken thighs
- 170 g chopped kale
- 2 red chili peppers, minced
- 2 onions, chopped
- 240 m tinned coconut milk
- 250 ml chicken stock
- 6 garlic cloves, minced
- 1 lemongrass stalk
- 45 ml freshly squeezed lime juice

DIRECTIONS:

1. Before getting started, be sure to remove the Cook & Crisp tray.
2. Mix the greens and kale and top with the onions, garlic, chili peppers, lemongrass, and chicken in the bottom of the pot. Pour in the chicken stock and coconut milk over all.
3. Close the lid and flip the SmartSwitch to AIR FRY/HOB. Select SLOW COOK, set temperature to LOW, and set time to 8 hours. Press START/STOP to begin cooking, until the chicken registers 75ºC on a food thermometer and the greens are soft.
4. Remove the lemongrass and discard. Gently stir in the lime juice and serve warm.

Salmon Vegetables Chowder

Prep Time: 15 minutes, Cook Time: 7½ hours, Serves: 8 to 10

INGREDIENTS:

- 900 g skinless salmon fillets
- 6 medium potatoes, cut into 5 cm pieces
- 4 large carrots, sliced
- 350 g sliced chestnut mushrooms
- 170 g shredded Swiss cheese
- 240 ml whole milk
- 2 L vegetable broth or fish stock
- 4 shallots, minced
- 3 garlic cloves, minced
- 2 tsp. dried dill weed

DIRECTIONS:

1. Before getting started, be sure to remove the Cook & Crisp tray.
2. Mix the potatoes, carrots, mushrooms, shallots, garlic, vegetable broth, and dill weed in the bottom of the pot.
3. Close the lid and flip the SmartSwitch to AIR FRY/HOB. Select SLOW COOK, set temperature to LOW, and set time to 7 hours. Press START/STOP to begin cooking, until the vegetables are soft.
4. Place the salmon fillets to the pot. Close the lid and cook on low for an additional 20 to 30 minutes, or until the salmon flakes when tested with a fork.
5. Gently stir the chowder to break up the salmon.
6. Pour in the milk and Swiss cheese and cover. Let the chowder sit for 10 minutes to let the cheese melt. Stir in the chowder and serve warm.

Italian Beetroots and Tomato

Prep Time: 17 minutes, Cook Time: 6 hours, Serves: 10

INGREDIENTS:

- 30 ml olive oil
- 10 medium beetroots, peeled and sliced
- 4 large tomatoes, seeded and chopped
- 2 onions, chopped
- 4 garlic cloves, minced
- 1 tsp. dried oregano leaves
- 1 tsp. dried basil leaves
- ½ tsp. salt

DIRECTIONS:

1. Before getting started, be sure to remove the Cook & Crisp tray.
2. Mix the beetroots, tomatoes, onions, and garlic in the bottom of the pot.
3. Add the olive oil and sprinkle with the dried herbs and salt. Toss to mix well.
4. Close the lid and flip the SmartSwitch to AIR FRY/HOB. Select SLOW COOK, set temperature to LOW, and set time to 6 hours. Press START/STOP to begin cooking, until the beetroots are soft.
5. Serve warm.

Tilapia and Spinach Risotto

Prep Time: 7 minutes, Cook Time: 4 hours 40 minutes, Serves: 4

INGREDIENTS:

- 360 g short-grain brown rice
- 6 (140 g each) tilapia fillets
- 225 g chestnut mushrooms, sliced
- 1.5 L vegetable broth or fish stock
- 90 g baby spinach leaves
- 2 onions, chopped
- 60 g grated Parmesan cheese
- 5 garlic cloves, minced
- 30 g unsalted butter
- 1 tsp. dried thyme leaves

DIRECTIONS:

1. Before getting started, be sure to remove the Cook & Crisp tray.
2. Mix the mushrooms, onions, garlic, rice, thyme, and vegetable broth in the bottom of the pot.
3. Close the lid and flip the SmartSwitch to AIR FRY/HOB. Select SLOW COOK, set temperature to LOW, and set time to 4 hours. Press START/STOP to begin cooking, until the rice is soft.
4. When the time is up, open the lid and place the fish on top of the rice. Close the lid and cook on low for another 30 minutes, or until the fish flakes when tested with a fork.
5. Gently place the fish into the risotto. Then put the baby spinach leaves.
6. Stir in the butter and cheese. Cover and allow to cook on low for 10 minutes, then Serve warm.

Honey Pork Chops and Carrot

Prep Time: 20 minutes, Cook Time: 8 hours, Serves: 8

INGREDIENTS:

- 8 (140-g) pork chops
- 4 large carrots, peeled and cut into chunks
- 125 ml chicken stock
- 2 onions, chopped
- 3 garlic cloves, minced
- 3 tbsps. grated fresh ginger root
- 45 ml honey
- ½ tsp. ground ginger
- ½ tsp. salt
- ⅛ tsp. freshly ground black pepper

DIRECTIONS:

1. Before getting started, be sure to remove the Cook & Crisp tray.
2. Mix the onions, garlic, and carrots in the bottom of the pot. Place the pork chops on top.
3. Mix the ginger root, honey, stock, ginger, salt, and pepper in a small bowl. Pour into the pot.
4. Close the lid and flip the SmartSwitch to AIR FRY/HOB. Select SLOW COOK, set temperature to LOW, and set time to 8 hours. Press START/STOP to begin cooking, until the pork is very soft.
5. Serve warm.

Sultana Carrot Pudding

Prep Time: 10 minutes, Cook Time: 6 hours, Serves: 12

INGREDIENTS:

- 375 g finely grated carrots
- 480 ml canned coconut milk
- 2 eggs, beaten
- 180 g chopped pecans
- 150 g golden sultanas
- 120 g coconut flour
- 120 g almond flour
- 100 g coconut sugar
- 1½ tsps. ground cinnamon
- 1 tsp. baking powder

DIRECTIONS:

1. Before getting started, be sure to remove the Cook & Crisp tray.
2. Mix all the ingredients in the bottom of the pot.
3. Close the lid and flip the SmartSwitch to AIR FRY/HOB. Select SLOW COOK, set temperature to LOW, and set time to 6 hours. Press START/STOP to begin cooking, until the pudding is set.
4. Serve hot, either plain or with softly double cream.

Curried Pork Chop with Pepper and Onion

Prep Time: 11 minutes, Cook Time: 8 hours, Serves: 4 to 6

INGREDIENTS:

- 8 (150-g) bone-in pork loin chops
- 2 red bell peppers, stemmed, seeded, and chopped
- 2 yellow bell peppers, stemmed, seeded, and chopped
- 2 onions, chopped
- 250 ml chicken stock
- 4 garlic cloves, minced
- 1 tbsp. curry powder
- 1 tbsp. grated fresh ginger root
- ½ tsp. salt

DIRECTIONS:

1. Before getting started, be sure to remove the Cook & Crisp tray.
2. Mix the onions, garlic, and bell peppers in the bottom of the pot. Put the pork chops to the pot, nestling them into the vegetables.
3. Mix the salt, curry powder, ginger root, and chicken stock in a small bowl, and pour the mixture into the pot.
4. Close the lid and flip the SmartSwitch to AIR FRY/HOB. Select SLOW COOK, set temperature to LOW, and set time to 7 hours. Press START/STOP to begin cooking, until the pork chops are soft.
5. Serve warm.

Traditional Chicken Provençal

Prep Time: 16 minutes, Cook Time: 8 hours, Serves: 10

INGREDIENTS:

- 1.4 kg boneless, skinless chicken thighs
- 4 large tomatoes, seeded and chopped
- 3 bulbs fennel, cored and sliced
- 2 onions, chopped
- 2 red bell peppers, stemmed, seeded, and chopped
- 6 garlic cloves, minced
- 30 g sliced black Greek olives
- 4 sprigs fresh thyme
- 1 bay leaf
- 30 ml lemon juice

DIRECTIONS:

1. Before getting started, be sure to remove the Cook & Crisp tray.
2. Mix all the ingredients in the bottom of the pot.
3. Close the lid and flip the SmartSwitch to AIR FRY/HOB. Select SLOW COOK, set temperature to LOW, and set time to 8 hours. Press START/STOP to begin cooking, until the chicken registers 75ºC on a food thermometer.
4. Remove the thyme stems and bay leaf and discard.
5. Serve warm.

Healthy Beef Stroganoff

Prep Time: 15 minutes, Cook Time: 8½ hours, Serves: 6 to 8

INGREDIENTS:

- 1.1 kg grass-fed chuck shoulder roast, trimmed of fat and cut into 5 cm cubes
- 5 large carrots, sliced
- 200 g sliced chestnut mushrooms
- 375 ml sour cream
- 500 ml beef stock
- 2 onions, chopped
- 8 garlic cloves, sliced
- 1 bay leaf
- 45 ml mustard
- 25 g cornflour
- 1 tsp. dried marjoram

DIRECTIONS:

1. Before getting started, be sure to remove the Cook & Crisp tray.
2. Mix the onions, mushrooms, carrots, garlic, and beef in the bottom of the pot.
3. Mix the beef stock and mustard in a medium bowl. Place the bay leaf and marjoram and pour into the pot.
4. Close the lid and flip the SmartSwitch to AIR FRY/HOB. Select SLOW COOK, set temperature to LOW, and set time to 8 hours. Press START/STOP to begin cooking, until the beef is very soft.
5. When the time is up, open the lid.
6. In a medium bowl, combine the sour cream and cornflour. Pour 240 ml of the liquid from the pot and whisk until blended well. Place the sour cream mixture to the pot.
7. Close the lid and cook on low for another 20 to 30 minutes, until the liquid has thickened.
8. Discard the bay leaf and serve warm.

APPENDIX 1: 30-DAY MEAL PLAN

Meal Plan	Breakfast	Lunch	Dinner	Snack/Dessert
Day-1	Cinnamon and Pecan Pie	Chicken with Pineapple and Peach	Scallops with Capers Sauce	Raspberry Wontons
Day-2	Creamy Cheese Soufflé	Lamb Loin Chops and Barley with Mushroom	Spiced Turkey Tenderloin	Classic Shortbread Fingers
Day-3	Icing Strawberry Cupcakes	Roasted Chicken Breast with Garlic	Cajun-Style Salmon Burgers	Dehydrated Kiwi Fruit
Day-4	Healthy Spinach Porridge	Sesame Chicken and Bean Rice	Glazed Brussels Sprouts	Easy Crispy Prawns
Day-5	Nutty Courgette Bread	Cheese Stuffed Bell Peppers	Breaded Flounder with Lemon	Apple Dumplings with Sultana
Day-6	Bacon and Spinach Cups	Lime Lamb and Scallions	Healthy Quinoa with Beef Strips	Chocolate Cherry Turnovers
Day-7	Crispy Cod Cakes with Salad Greens	Honey Sriracha Chicken Wings	Beef Loin with Herbs	Dehydrated Strawberry Slices
Day-8	Sultana Carrot Pudding	Citrus Pork Roast and Spinach Rice	Air Fried Chicken Tenders	Beef Steak Fingers
Day-9	Parmesan Sausage Muffins	Garlic Kimchi Chicken and Cabbage	Beef and Carrot Meatballs	Tasty Mixed Nuts
Day-10	Pear and Apple Crisp	Herbed Beef	Teriyaki Salmon with Brown Rice	Sweet and Spicy Pepper Beef Jerky

Meal Plan	Breakfast	Lunch	Dinner	Snack/Dessert
Day-11	Honey Pumpkin Bread	Pork Tenderloin with Bell Peppers	Chicken Pomegranate Stew	Walnut Chocolate Cake
Day-12	Prawn Burgers	Beef and Spinach Rolls	Beef Meatballs and Pea Rice	Almond-Crusted Chicken Nuggets
Day-13	Icing Strawberry Cupcakes	Jerk Chicken Leg Quarters	Lamb Chops with Bulb Garlic	Chilli Fingerling Potatoes
Day-14	Vegan Quinoa Egg Casserole	Simple Mexican Pork Chops	Cajun-Style Salmon Burgers	Beef Steak Fingers
Day-15	Crispy Cod Cakes with Salad Greens	Chinese Pork and Mushroom Pasta	Moroccan Beef Tagine and Carrot	Classic Shortbread Fingers
Day-16	Creamy Cheese Soufflé	Salmon Vegetables Chowder	Air Fried Baby Back Ribs	Chocolate Cherry Turnovers
Day-17	Bacon and Spinach Cups	Breaded Hake and Green Beans Meal	Buttered Striploin Steak	Easy Crispy Prawns
Day-18	Parmesan Sausage Muffins	Little Bay Yellow Curry	Mustard Lamb Loin Chops and Broccoli Pasta	Tasty Mixed Nuts
Day-19	Prawn Burgers	Cranberry Beef Stir-Fry with Veggies	Ginger Lentil Stew	Peach Brown Betty with Cranberries
Day-20	Pear and Apple Crisp	Chinese Chicken Drumsticks with Pasta	Thai Basil Pork Bowls	Smoky Salmon Jerky

Meal Plan	Breakfast	Lunch	Dinner	Snack/Dessert
Day-21	Icing Strawberry Cupcakes	Beef and Carrot Meatballs	Balsamic Asparagus with Almond	Spicy Sriracha Turkey Jerky
Day-22	Vegan Quinoa Egg Casserole	Hoisin Tofu	Pulled Pork with Mushroom Polenta	Almond-Crusted Chicken Nuggets
Day-23	Nutty Courgette Bread	Jerk Chicken Leg Quarters	Glazed Brussels Sprouts	Raspberry Wontons
Day-24	Honey Pumpkin Bread	Beef Short Ribs with Cauliflower Rice	Herbed Radishes	Walnut Chocolate Cake
Day-25	Creamy Cheese Soufflé	Sichuan Pork and Bell Pepper with Peanuts	Honey Sriracha Chicken Wings	Apple Dumplings with Sultana
Day-26	Cinnamon and Pecan Pie	Chili Breaded Pork Chops	Spicy Prawn and Broccoli Pasta	Sweet and Sour Chicken Jerky
Day-27	Parmesan Sausage Muffins	Scallops with Capers Sauce	Spiced Turkey Tenderloin	Chilli Fingerling Potatoes
Day-28	Healthy Spinach Porridge	Buttermilk Paprika Chicken	Simple Lamb Chops with Quinoa and Chickpea	Tangy Dehydrated Mango Slices
Day-29	Bacon and Spinach Cups	Pork Tenderloin with Bell Peppers	Air Fried Chicken Tenders	Classic Shortbread Fingers
Day-30	Sultana Carrot Pudding	Jamaican Chicken Drumsticks with Spinach Couscous	Beef and Spinach Rolls	Tasty Mixed Nuts

APPENDIX 2: NINJA SPEEDI TIMETABLE

Steam Air Fry Chart

INGREDIENT	AMOUNT	PREPARATION	WATER	ORIENTATION	TEMP	COOK TIME
POULTRY						
Chicken breasts	2 (175g each)	None	125ml	Top	190°C	15-20 mins
Chicken breasts, breaded	4 (175g each)	None	125ml	Top	190°C	18-20 mins
Chicken drumsticks	1kg	None	125ml	Top	210°C	25-30 mins
Chicken thighs (bone in)	1kg	None	125ml	Top	190°C	20-25 mins
Chicken thighs (boneless)	4 (100-125g each)	None	125ml	Top	190°C	15-18 mins
Chicken wings	500g	None	125ml	Bottom	220°C	15 mins
Whole chicken	2-2.5kg	Trussed	250ml	Bottom	180°C	60-80 mins
Turkey breast	1.4-2.4kg	None	250ml	Bottom	180°C	45-55 mins
BEEF						
Topside	1.5kg	None	250ml	Bottom	180°C	45 mins for medium rare
Rolled rib	1.5kg	None	250ml	Bottom	180°C	30-32 mins for medium rare
PORK						
Pork chops	4 thick-cut, bone-in (250g each)	Bone in	125ml	Top	190°C	25-30 mins
Pork chops	4 boneless (100-125g each)	Boneless	125ml	Top	190°C	20-25 mins
Pork loin	1kg	None	250ml	Bottom	180°C	35-40 mins
LAMB						
Leg of lamb	1.5kg	None	250ml	Bottom	180°C	37-40 mins
FISH						
Cod	4 (150g each)	None	125ml	Top	220°C	9-12 mins
Salmon	4 (150g each)	None	65ml	Top	220°C	7-10 mins

*NOTE: Crisper tray position varies, as specified in chart. Steam will take approximately 4-10 minutes to build.

Steam Air Fry Chart

INGREDIENT	AMOUNT	PREPARATION	WATER	ORIENTATION	TEMP	COOK TIME
FROZEN POULTRY						
Chicken breasts	4 (175g each)	None	250ml	Top	200°C	15-20 mins
Chicken drumsticks	1kg	None	125ml	Top	180°C	20-25 mins
Chicken thighs	1kg	None	125ml	Top	200°C	20-22 mins
Chicken wings	500g	None	125ml	Bottom	220°C	15 mins
FROZEN BEEF						
Steak, sirloin	2 (225g each)	None	250ml	Top	180°C	12-18 mins
FROZEN FISH						
Salmon	4 (120g each)	None	65ml	Top	220°C	7-10 mins
Cod	4 (120g each)	None	125ml	Top	220°C	10-15 mins
FROZEN PORK						
Pork chops with bone	2 (250g each)	None	125ml	Bottom	190°C	23-28 mins
Sausages	450g	None	125ml	Bottom	190°C	10-12 mins
VEGETABLES						
Beetroot	1kg	Peel, cut into 1.25cm cubes	125ml	Bottom	200°C	30-35 mins
Broccoli	400g	Whole, remove stem	125ml	Bottom	210°C	15-20 mins
Brussels sprouts	1kg	Cut in half, trim ends	125ml	Bottom	220°C	10-12 mins
Butternut squash	1kg	Cut in half, deseed	125ml	Bottom	190°C	22-25 mins
Carrots	1kg	Peel, cut into 1.25cm rounds	125ml	Bottom	200°C	22-28 mins
Parsnip	500g	Cut into 2.5cm pieces	125ml	Bottom	200°C	30-35 mins
Potatoes, King Edward/Maris Piper/Russet	1kg	Cut into 2.5cm wedges	125ml	Bottom	220°C	30-35 mins
	4, 800g	Whole	125ml	Bottom	200°C	25-30 mins
Sweet potatoes	1kg	Cut into 2.5cm cubes	125ml	Bottom	200°C	20 mins

*NOTE: Crisper tray position varies, as specified in chart. Steam will take approximately 4-10 minutes to build.

Air Fry Chart for the Crisper Tray, bottom position

INGREDIENT	AMOUNT	PREPARATION	OIL	TEMP	COOK TIME
VEGETABLES					
Asparagus	250g	Trim stems	2 tsp	200°C	7-8 mins
Bell peppers	4 (750g)	Whole	None	200°C	20 mins
Cauliflower	400g	Cut in 2.5-5cm florets	1 tbsp	200°C	12-14 mins
Corn on the cob	4 ears (1kg)	Whole ears, husk removed	1 tbsp	200°C	12-15 mins
Courgette	500g	Cut in quarters lengthwise, then into 2.5cm pieces	1 tbsp	200°C	11-12 mins
Green beans	350g	Trimmed	1 tbsp	200°C	7-10 mins
Kale for chips	400g	Torn in pieces, stems removed	None	150°C	8-12 mins
Mushrooms	300g	Wipe, quarter	1 tbsp	200°C	7-8 mins
Potatoes, King Edward/Maris Piper/Russets	500g	Hand cut chips, thin	½-3 tbsp	200°C	18-22 mins
	500g	Hand cut chips, thick	½-3 tbsp	200°C	20-22 mins
Potatoes, sweet	1kg	Cut into 2.5cm cubes	1 tbsp	200°C	14-16 mins
BEEF					
Burgers	4 (125g each)	1.5-1.75cm thick	None	190°C	10 mins
Steak	2 (225g each)	None	Brushed with oil	200°C	8-12 mins
PORK					
Bacon	6 rashers, (200g)	Lay rashers evenly over tray	None	170°C	10 mins
Gammon steak	1 (225g)	Whole	None	200°C	10-12 mins
Sausages	8 (450g)	None	None	200°C	7-8 mins

*TIP When using Air Fry, add 5 minutes to the suggested cook time for the unit to preheat before you add ingredients.

Air Fry Chart for the Crisper Tray, bottom position

INGREDIENT	AMOUNT	PREPARATION	OIL	TEMP	COOK TIME
FROZEN FOODS					
Chicken nuggets	380g	None	None	200°C	10 mins
Fish fillets (battered)	440g	None	None	200°C	14 mins
Fish fingers	10 (280g)	None	None	200°C	9-10 mins
Hash browns	8 (360g)	None	None	200°C	14 mins
Roast potatoes	700g	None	None	200°C	25-30 mins
Mozzarella sticks	360g	None	None	200°C	6-7 mins
Onion rings	300g	None	None	200°C	10-12 mins
Scampi	9 jumbo pieces (230g)	None	None	200°C	7 mins
Sweet potato fries	500g	None	None	200°C	15 mins
Veggie burgers	4 (350g)	None	None	190°C	14 mins
Veggie sausages	6 (270g)	None	None	200°C	7-8 mins
FROZEN CHIPS					
Light straight chips	500g	None	None	200°C	14 mins
Chunky chips	500g	None	None	200°C	17 mins
Crinkle cut chips	500g	None	None	200°C	16 mins
French fries	500g	None	None	180°C	14 mins
Gastro chips	700g	None	None	200°C	18-20 mins
Potato wedges	650g	None	None	200°C	15 mins
Skin-on chips	500g	None	None	200°C	16-17 mins
FISH & SEAFOOD					
Fishcakes	2 (150g each)	None	None	200°C	8-10 mins
Prawns	16 jumbo	Raw, whole, tails on	1 tbsp	200°C	7-10 mins

*TIP When using Air Fry, add 5 minutes to the suggested cook time for the unit to preheat before you add ingredients.

Steam Chart for the Crisper Tray, bottom position

INGREDIENT	AMOUNT	PREPARATION	LIQUID	COOK TIME
VEGETABLES				
Asparagus	250g	Whole spears	250ml	5-7 mins
Broccoli	300g	Cut into 2.5-5cm florets	250ml	5-9 mins
Brussels sprouts	400g	Whole, trimmed	250ml	10-15 mins
Butternut squash	500g	Peeled, cut into 2.5cm cubes	250ml	10-15 mins
Carrots	500g	Peeled, cut into 2.5cm pieces	250ml	10-15 mins
Cauliflower	400g	Peeled, cut into 2.5-5cm florets	250ml	5-10 mins
Corn on the cob	4 ears	Whole, husks removed	250ml	8-10 mins
Green beans	200g	Whole, trimmed	250ml	8-12 mins
Potatoes	500g	Peeled, cut into 2.5cm pieces	325ml	12-17 mins
Potatoes, baby new	500g	Whole pieces	325ml	15-20 mins
Sweet potatoes	500g	Cut into 1.25cm cubes	250ml	8-14 mins

Dehydrate Chart for the Crisper Tray, bottom position

INGREDIENT	PREPARATION	TEMP	DEHYDRATE TIME
FRUITS & VEGETABLES			
Apple chips	Cut into 3mm slices, remove core, rinse in lemon water, pat dry	60°C	7-8 hrs
Bananas	Peel, cut into 3mm slices	60°C	8-10 hrs
Fresh herbs	Rinse, pat dry, remove stems	60°C	4-6 hrs
Ginger root	Cut into 3mm slices	60°C	6 hrs
Mangoes	Peel, cut into 3mm slices, remove stone	60°C	6-8 hrs
Mushrooms	Clean with soft brush or wipe with damp kitchen paper	60°C	6-8 hrs
Pineapple	Peel, cut into 3mm-1.25cm slices, core removed	60°C	6-8 hrs
Strawberries	Cut in half or into 1.25cm slices	60°C	6-8 hrs
Tomatoes	Cut into 3mm slices; steam if planning to rehydrate	60°C	6-8 hrs
MEAT, POULTRY, FISH			
Beef, chicken, salmon jerky	Cut into 6mm slices, marinate overnight	70°C	5-7 hrs

*TIP Most fruits and vegetables take between 6 and 8 hours (at 60°C) to dehydrate; meats take between 5 and 7 hours (at 70°C). The longer you dehydrate your ingredients, the crispier they will be.

APPENDIX 3: RECIPES INDEX

A

APPLE
Apple Dumplings with Sultana	39
Pear and Apple Crisp	47

ARTICHOKE
Crispy Artichoke Hearts	40

ASPARAGUS
Balsamic Asparagus with Almond	43
8-Hour Dehydrated Asparagus	52
Sesame Asparagus	62

AUBERGINE
Roasted Aubergine Slices	43
Crispy Dehydrated Aubergine Slices	52

B

BABY BACK RIB
Air Fried Baby Back Ribs	37

BACON
Bacon and Spinach Cups	26
Potato and Bacon Nuggets	38

BANANA
Peanut Butter Banana Bread	28
Crispy Dehydrated Banana Chips	53

BEEF
Beef Meatballs and Pea Rice	7
Beef and Carrot Meatballs	20

BEEF BRISKET
Mustard Beef Brisket	69

BEEF CUBE STEAK
Beef Steak Fingers	36

BEEF EYE OF ROUND
Sweet and Spicy Pepper Beef Jerky	56

BEEF LOIN
Beef Loin with Herbs	48

BEEF SHORT RIB
Beef Short Ribs with Cauliflower Rice	8

BEEF SHOULDER ROAST
Healthy Beef Stroganoff	74

BEEF SIRLOIN ROAST
Moroccan Beef Tagine and Carrot	69

BEEF STEAK
Healthy Quinoa with Beef Strips	7
Herbed Beef	38

BEEF STEW MEAT
Cranberry Beef Stir-Fry with Veggies	59

BEETROOT
Italian Beetroots and Tomato	72

BELL PEPPER
Cheese Stuffed Bell Peppers	19

BROCCOLI
Cheese Broccoli Bites	16

BRUSSELS SPROUTS
Glazed Brussels Sprouts	23
Crunchy Dehydrated Brussels Sprouts	52
Brussels Sprouts with Pistachios	65

C

CARROT
Crunchy Dehydrated Carrot Slices	54
Sultana Carrot Pudding	73

CHERRY
Chocolate Cherry Turnovers	32

CHICKEN
Garlic Kimchi Chicken and Cabbage	64

CHICKEN BREAST
Sesame Chicken and Bean Rice	12
Chicken with Pineapple and Peach	23
Buttermilk Paprika Chicken	36
Almond-Crusted Chicken Nuggets	39
Air Fried Chicken Tenders	40
Roasted Chicken Breast with Garlic	45
Sweet and Sour Chicken Jerky	57
Little Bay Yellow Curry	62
Chicken Breast with Artichokes and Bell Pepper	69

CHICKEN DRUMSTICK
Jamaican Chicken Drumsticks with Spinach Couscous	11
Chinese Chicken Drumsticks with Pasta	12

CHICKEN LEG
Chicken Pomegranate Stew	64

CHICKEN LEG QUARTER
Jerk Chicken Leg Quarters	35

CHICKEN THIGH
Thai Chicken with Greens — 71
Traditional Chicken Provençal — 74
CHICKEN WING
Honey Sriracha Chicken Wings — 20
COD
Paprika Cod — 16
Crunchy Cod Nuggets — 18
Crispy Cod Cakes with Salad Greens — 44
New England Fried Chips and Fried Fish — 59
CORNED BEEF
Corned Beef — 61
COURGETTE
Nutty Courgette Bread — 29

D-F

DRAGON FRUIT
Dehydrated Dragon Fruit — 54
FINGERLING POTATO
Chilli Fingerling Potatoes — 41
FLANK STEAK
Beef and Spinach Rolls — 27
FLOUNDER
Breaded Flounder with Lemon — 34

H-K

HAKE
Breaded Hake and Green Beans Meal — 13
KALE
Vegan Quinoa Egg Casserole — 70
KIWI
Dehydrated Kiwi Fruit — 55

L

LAMB CHOP
Simple Lamb Chops with Quinoa and Chickpea — 8
Lamb Chops with Bulb Garlic — 48
LAMB LEG
Sichuan Cumin-Spiced Lamb — 66
LAMB LOIN CHOP
Mustard Lamb Loin Chops and Broccoli Pasta — 9
Lamb Loin Chops and Barley with Mushroom — 9
LAMB TENDERLOIN
Lime Lamb and Scallions — 65

M-O

MANGO
Tangy Dehydrated Mango Slices — 53
OLIVE
Crunchy Dehydrated Olives — 55
ORANGE LENTIL
Ginger Lentil Stew — 61
OYSTER MUSHROOM
Mushroom and Bell Pepper Pizza — 25

P

PEACH
Peach Brown Betty with Cranberries — 68
PEANUT
Tasty Mixed Nuts — 50
PECAN
Vanilla Pecan Pie — 31
Cinnamon and Pecan Pie — 47
PEPPERONI
Portabella Pizza Treat — 22
PINK SALMON
Cajun-Style Salmon Burgers — 17
PORK
Sichuan Pork and Bell Pepper with Peanuts — 60
Thai Basil Pork Bowls — 63
PORK CHOP
Chinese Pork and Mushroom Pasta — 10
Simple Mexican Pork Chops — 46
Chili Breaded Pork Chops — 46
Honey Pork Chops and Carrot — 73
PORK LOIN CHOP
Curried Pork Chop with Pepper and Onion — 73
PORK LOIN ROAST
Citrus Pork Roast and Spinach Rice — 10
PORK SHOULDER
Pulled Pork with Mushroom Polenta — 11
PORK TENDERLOIN
Pork Tenderloin with Bell Peppers — 18

PRAWN
Spicy Prawn and Broccoli Pasta	14
Prawn Burgers	29
Easy Crispy Prawns	37
Salt and Pepper Prawn	60

R

RADISH
Herbed Radishes	35

RASPBERRY
Raspberry Wontons	34

S

SALMON
Teriyaki Salmon with Brown Rice	13
Easy Roasted Salmon	44
Smoky Salmon Jerky	56
Salmon Vegetables Chowder	71

SAUSAGE
Italian Sausage Meatballs	21
Parmesan Sausage Muffins	28

SCALLOP
Scallops with Capers Sauce	17

SPINACH
Eggless Spinach and Bacon Quiche	30
Healthy Spinach Porridge	70

STRAWBERRY
Icing Strawberry Cupcakes	27
Dehydrated Strawberry Slices	55

STRIPLOIN STEAK
Buttered Striploin Steak	47

SWEETCORN ON THE COB
Buttered Sweetcorn on the Cob	19

T

TILAPIA
Tilapia and Spinach Risotto	72

TOFU
Hoisin Tofu	63

TOMATO
6-Hour Dehydrated Tomatoes	51

TUNA
Savory Tuna Cakes	25

TURKEY
Cheddar Turkey Burgers	21

TURKEY BREAST
Spicy Sriracha Turkey Jerky	57

TURKEY BREAST TENDERLOIN
Spiced Turkey Tenderloin	45

W

WALNUT
Walnut Chocolate Cake	31

Printed in Great Britain
by Amazon